IS SOUTH DAKOTA HAUNTED?

- Does **Seth Bullock** haunt the Bullock Hotel in Deadwood?

- Do the ghosts of **Wild Bill Hickok, Calamity Jane, Potato Creek Johnny,** and **Preacher Smith** haunt the Mount Moriah Cemetery?

- Does **Crazy Horse** haunt the Crazy Horse Memorial?

- Does **Dorothy Gale**, from *The Wizard of Oz*, haunt a castle in Aberdeen?

- Do **Ma and Pa Ingalls**, from *Little House on the Prairie,* haunt their homestead in De Smet?

- Does **Jesse James** haunt Devil's Gulch in Garretson?

- Do the ghosts of prospector **"Wild Horse" Harry Hardin** and his burro **Sugar Babe** haunt the Mountain View Cemetery?

- Does **Hooky Jack** haunt a restaurant in Rapid City?

- Does **Judge Amidon** haunt a monument in Sioux Falls?

Here's the definitive road guide for finding the ghosts of coal miners, prostitutes, ranchers, gunslingers, gamblers, prospectors, outlaws, lawmen, soldiers, warriors, bankers, preachers, actors, bushwhackers, roughriders, doctors, and a wide variety of historical and colorful characters from South Dakota's exciting past.

What people are saying about this book

"There is a superabundance of travel guides to the sights in South Dakota, but paranormal investigators Lewis and Fisk have produced the first and only guide to the shadowlands of our state."

Ted Hustead - Wall Drug

****

"First Lady Bess Truman once said, 'Now about those ghosts. I'm sure they're here and I'm not half so alarmed at meeting up with any of them as I am at having to meet the live nuts I have to see every day.' And that's the beauty of this book – it may lead you to both. For the adventurer or the arm-chair traveler, this work is a joy to read, capturing the pioneer spirit of South Dakota and cornering the lingering ghosts in whose footsteps we walk each night."

T.D. Griffith - publisher of *Deadwood Magazine* and author of *Insider's Guide to South Dakota's Black Hills & Badlands*

****

"Want to go where the willies are? Then you need the **South Dakota Road Guide to Haunted Locations** *by Chad Lewis and Terry Fisk. Lewis and Fisk have traveled the state in their ghost-mobile to locate, photograph, research and test out every haunted cemetery, restaurant, theater and outhouse in the state. The comprehensive information presented is almost an overload of otherworldly riches, perfect for either the gonzo road-tripper or the stay-at-home reader. Highly recommended!"*

Linda S. Godfrey - author of *Hunting the American Werewolf, The Beast of Bray Road, Weird Michigan,* and co-author of *Weird Wisconsin.*

THE
SOUTH
DAKOTA
ROAD GUIDE
TO
HAUNTED
LOCATIONS

THE
SOUTH
DAKOTA
ROAD GUIDE
TO
HAUNTED
LOCATIONS

By Chad Lewis & Terry Fisk

Research Publishing Company
A Division of Unexplained Research, LLC

Library of Congress Control Number: 2006903787
ISBN: 978-0-9762099-3-5

Printed in the United States by Documation

Unexplained Research Publishing Company
A Division of Unexplained Research LLC
P.O. Box 2173, Eau Claire, WI 54702-2173
Email: info@unexplainedresearch.com
www.unexplainedresearch.com

Cover Design: Terry Fisk
Back Cover Photo: Rob Mattison

DEDICATION

I dedicate this book to my brother, Todd Lewis, for igniting my interest in the paranormal by scaring me with his ghost encounters from our childhood.

—Chad

I dedicate this book to my beloved siblings, Cindy, Rick, and Randy, and to the fond memories of us playing on haunted Casper's Island.

—Terry

TABLE OF CONTENTS

1 - Central South Dakota   1

2 - Eastern South Dakota   25

3 - Northern South Dakota   71

4 - Western South Dakota   123

PREFACE

Corrections. Although we have made every effort to be certain this road guide is reliable and accurate, things inevitably change and errors are made. We appreciate it when readers contact us so we can revise future editions of the book.

Updates. If you have a paranormal experience at one of these locations, please report it to us. We recommend that you keep a journal, carefully recording dates, times, locations, and what happened.

Additions. Due to lack of space, many locations had to be left out the book. We do intend to publish a second volume. Please write and let us know of any South Dakota locations that you feel should have been included in this travel guide.

Warning. Be respectful of both the living and the dead. Several communities have had problems with people who go to these locations only to party and cause mischief. Cemeteries have been desecrated; private property has been vandalized; grounds have been littered; and buildings have been broken into.

If you do decide to check out any of the locations for yourself, please make sure that you have permission if it is private property and obey all applicable laws. Under most ordinances, cemeteries are only open from sunrise to sunset.

We will not be held responsible for any persons who decide to conduct their own investigations or for those who choose to break laws.

Disclaimer. The places listed in the book have neither been proved nor disproved to be haunted. Their inclusion in the book is based on the anecdotal reports we have received from numerous individuals. This book is for reference purposes only.

FOREWORD

He pulled the weathered brown boots over his faded blue jeans, and stood up.

The room was dim, only lit by one burning lantern on the desk and a small bedroom window facing north. He looked at the cross hanging over the unmade bed as he strapped on his gun around his trim waist. He pulled it out of the leather and counted the brass bullets, six. The tall cowboy gazed back at the wooden cross one more time as he pulled the black cowboy hat over his long shaggy brown hair. The tight rim of the hat held back the beads of sweat that were now forming. This could be his last day, he thought. He took one long look at his sweetheart's picture on the desk and walked out the bedroom door. He walked down the short hall to the bar where just last night fate brought him to this point. A showdown with one of the notorious gunslingers in the west, Wild Texas Jake Thorn. The late morning light lit the empty bar. It was nothing like the night before where it was full of cow rustlers and poker players. Wild Jake told the cowboy to meet him in front of the saloon at high noon, and that is just what the cowboy did. In the West, men died for honor especially for a woman's hand. This was no exception; he had to fight Thorn or be branded a coward for the rest of his life. The cowboy walked out of the swinging doors to find the townsfolk gathered round but they were easily scattered as soon as his cowboy boots hit the dirt street. Wild Jake was standing on the other side of the street like he was leaning on something, and sneering at the scared cowboy. The cowboy faced the notorious gunslinger and started walking toward him. Texas Jake, handsome and rugged was found the night before with the cowboy's girl in his arms; nothing less than a showdown would do to settle the score. A few steps more and a gunshot rang out. Only one. Wild Jake's gun still had the smoke curling from its silver end as the cowboy hit the dusty ground.

Some say to this day that it was not a fair fight, but the cowboy was dead and Texas Jake got the girl. Others say that the cowboy still roams the streets trying to find his love, and others will testify that he still straps on the six shooter and walks South Dakota looking for Thorn, and even few say that they still see him die.

The South Dakota Road Guide to Haunted Locations brings you to the edge of eerie legends, scary folktales, and haunted locations. Chad and Terry bring you to the brink of wonder with this fascinating road map of hauntings and scary places. They bring in years of experience to keep the most skeptical minds wondering, could there really be ghosts? Find out for yourself as you bring your whole family to South Dakota, not just to find gold and Wall Drug. But maybe you could be one of the lucky few to find yourself a ghost. Take this book on your next vacation as you go from place to place living the past with wonder and awe, as you ask yourself if there could really be spirits of the dead.

So the next time you take a trip to Mount Rushmore and the Badlands take Chad and Terry's book with you. Take a little side trip and see for yourself. Could there really be a cowboy searching for his love? But I warn you, you better watch your step, partner, or you could be caught in the next shootout with Wild Texas Jake.

Michael Thomas Coffield
Author of *The 13th Planet: Coming out of Darkness*

ACKNOWLEDGMENTS

We would like to thank Chris Belisle, Nisa Giaquinto, Jay & Laura Tench, Jim Tench, Sarah Szymanski, and Jeannine Fisk for assisting us with the research and production of this book.

A special thank you is extended to Paul Stucklen.

We also want to thank the many people who provided us with cases, directions, and personal accounts.

INTRODUCTIONS

The cure for boredom is curiosity. There is no cure for curiosity.

--Dorothy Parker

Why are you doing a book on haunted locations in South Dakota? It was the one question that I was most often asked while preparing for this book. Not being one to settle on a simple "why not" response, I needed to go into a little more detail. I finally explained that I simply love adventures. In my eyes, the more wacky and weird the adventure turned out to be, the more fun I had while on it. I have traveled to many paranormal hotspots around the world. Throughout my travels I have searched for the Loch Ness monster in Scotland, scoured Transylvania for vampires, hiked the rain-forests of Puerto Rico for the chupacabras, and even explored the remote countryside of Ireland hoping to glimpse a gnome. Yet, the idea of hopping into a car equipped with a few maps, some food, and an abundance of excitement truly is my favorite adventure. The thrill of setting off to explore a new state, meeting the people, seeing the terrain, learning the subtle cultural differences, and most of all, uncovering the ghosts, is the ultimate journey for me.

A long car trip out on the open road where anything can happen makes one feel like a pioneer of days past, and what better place to be a pioneer than South Dakota? The state has a long history of embracing the pioneer spirit. From the early days of the gold rush to the yearly Sturgis bike rally, South Dakota is full of unique characters. However, to most of the nation South Dakota seems like a quiet sparsely populated state where nothing spectacular ever seems to happen. It was with this misconception that we decided that the ghosts of South Dakota had been dormant far too long, and it was time to show that South Dakota's reputation could not be further from the truth.

Those of you who live in the state certainly know, and those of you just passing through will quickly find out, that South Dakota provides enough amazing activities to please even the pickiest of travelers. Filled with the diversity of the Badlands, Mt. Rushmore, Crazy Horse Memorial, Custer State Park, and the Black Hills, South Dakota is truly a national treasure.

In addition to the natural destinations, South Dakota also provides some of the best roadside attractions in the US ranging from Wall Drug and the Corn Palace, to the Dinosaur Park, and Deadwood. With so much to see and do, it is no wonder over three million tourists travel to the state each and every year. Yet most people may pass through, visit, eat, or even spend the night in these haunted locations and not even realize it. This haunted guide looks to change that.

Just as the famous explorers Lewis and Clark did over 200 years ago, we too set out on an adventure to explore the unknown territory in the state. The only difference was that our adventure consisted of seeking ghosts, spirits, and the most haunted locations the state had to offer. Even though we were armed with many modern day conveniences not available in the day of Lewis and Clark, we still found ourselves just as speechless and amazed by the beauty of the state as they were. It was quite the experience to set foot on the same land where Lewis and Clark, Crazy Horse, Wild Bill Hickok, and Seth Bullock once stood. Yet we wrote this guide to provide you the chance to not only stand on the same ground as South

Dakota's past residents, but to come face to face with many of their ghosts.

While researching the state we found almost as many haunted locations as there are signs for Wall Drug. Yet, we realize that paranormal investigations are sometimes hard and just because haunted locations are abundant, it doesn't mean they are easy to visit. With a plethora of wrong turns, urban legends, misinformation, and ghosts that have not appeared in over 100 years, we understand that many people would rather just hunker down and watch a scary movie. Yet while it may be fun to vicariously venture into a haunted cemetery through a TV show, it is a completely different matter when you are actually there. You cannot simply change the channel when you spot shadowy figures lurking from gravestone to gravestone, and the mute button will not aid you when the ghostly wails of a mother eternally searching for her lost child haunt your eardrums.

Rest assured that this book will certainly make your trip to any haunted location as easy as spotting a South Dakota prairie dog because we have done all the legwork. We tracked down the most haunted locations, dug up their history, sought out the witnesses, unearthed the ghost lore, conducted the investigations, and provided the directions for you. We have even included pictures of each site for those of you looking to vicariously visit these places through the comfort and safety of your own home.

Many paranormal books delve into great detail about the history of ghosts, speculating on the various theories of ghosts and haunted places. For this introduction, I have intentionally skipped the basic ghost history, as I feel this book is just as much about adventure, as it is about ghosts. For me, both paranormal research and adventure go hand in hand, the two are inseparable.

Yet this book is only the beginning; the adventure is now firmly in your hands. Literally. Take this guide with you as you witness ghosts roaming cemeteries, pick up vanishing hitchhikers, see phantom animals, or stay overnight in a haunted hotel. The possibilities are endless, and so are the experiences that you are bound to have on your journey. You will see parts of the state that you have never seen, you may meet some odd people, see many odd things, but most of all, you will have an adventure. No one on their deathbed wished that their life had been less exciting. Now take this guide, grab a friend, and set out on your paranormal journey.

Good luck on your adventure,

Chad Lewis

Where there is an open mind there will always be a frontier.

--Charles F. Kettering

When my father turned 18, he and a friend drove out to South Dakota. The state left such a lasting impression on him that years later, after starting a family, he and my mother bought a pop-up tent trailer and twice took us four kids to South Dakota for a vacation. When I was in my early twenties, I traveled to South Dakota with a couple of friends. Eventually, just like my father, I bought a pop-up tent trailer and took my own family on vacation there—visiting many of the same attractions that my father had taken me to. Most likely my children will carry on the tradition with their little ones.

Although vacations can sometimes be stressful experiences, I consistently found the beauty of South Dakota to be tranquilizing. The spirituality of its natural environment is invigorating and conducive to good health. Even the South Dakota state song lauds this salubrious quality: "Hail! South Dakota, A great state of the land, *Health*, wealth and beauty, That's what makes her grand." George Ayres, an earlier frontiersman, claimed "The climate in the Black Hills is so damn healthy that you have to kill a man to start a cemetery." Indeed, during the frontier days of the Wild West, there was a lot of bloodshed, and the number of cemeteries in Dakota Territory rapidly grew overnight.

The end of the American frontier was declared in 1890. By the 1960s it was believed that space was the next and final frontier. There is, however, a frontier much closer to home. It is the borderland, the fringe, the twilight zone between life and death. It is the realm of the restless dead. For whatever reasons, these souls are reputedly trapped between this life and the afterlife; unable to move forward. For centuries, Native Americans have been aware of the spirits and ghosts that inhabit the South Dakota region. When the white settlers moved into the territory, they, likewise, realized the land was permeated by a supernatural presence.

Some have made the comparison that the Lewis and Clark expedition explored the physical landscape of South Dakota; now, two-hundred years later, the Lewis and Fisk expedition has explored the metaphysical landscape of the state. Over a period of several months, Chad and I traveled to every corner of South Dakota, mapping out this paranormal frontier, and searching for its strangest and most haunted locations.

We've fearlessly trudged through the Badlands and wilderness in search of unusual creatures, such as the "little people" at Spirit Mound, the spider imp *Iktomi* at Devil's Gulch, the Devil at McLaughlin, and spook lights, thunderbirds, and Bigfoot at Sica Hollow. We've even investigated reports of phantom dogs at Bear Butte and phantom mules at Keystone.

Many of the cases we've collected and investigated are directly related to the history of the state, so we've included a chronology for the reader to better understand the interconnectedness of the people and events that we talk about.

If you have an open mind and a desire for adventure, then get out there and explore this wide-open frontier. Don't let your fear hold you back. A famous movie cowboy once offered the definition that "courage is being scared to death—but saddling up anyway."

Even if you don't come face-to-face with a ghost, you will meet up with the spirit of South Dakota's rich history and be able to experience firsthand the awe of its mysteries and legends.

Enjoy!

Terry Fisk

CHRONOLOGY OF SOUTH DAKOTA HISTORY

Indian Territory
Native Americans lived in this area for at least 25,000 years. In the 1800s, the Arikara (Ree) and Sioux (Dakota, Lakota, and Nakota) were the dominant tribes. By the 1830s the Arikara, driven out by the Sioux, settled in what is now North Dakota.

1682 Louisiana Territory
Although Indians had lived here for centuries, René-Robert Cavelier claimed this land, including present-day South Dakota, for France.

1743 Verendrye Expedition
French-Canadian brothers, Chevalier and Louis Verendrye explored this area and buried a lead plate on a hill proclaiming this land for Louis XV, King of France. The brothers misled the Indians, telling them the plate was to commemorate their meeting and the desire to live together in harmony. The Indians, unable to read French, had no idea the brothers were declaring the land to be the property of France. In 1913, the plate was discovered by high school students (see page 5).

1803 Louisiana Purchase
The United States acquired the half billion acre territory from France. Part of this land would eventually become the state of South Dakota.

1804 Lewis and Clark Expedition
President Thomas Jefferson sent Meriwether Lewis and William Clark to explore the newly-acquired region. Following the Missouri River, Lewis and Clark made stops at Spirit Mound (see page 68) near Vermillion on August 25 and at La Frambois Island (see page 21) in Pierre (pronounced *peer*) on September 25. At the mouth of the Teton River they raised the first American flag in South Dakota.

1817 LaFramboise Trading Post
Joseph LaFramboise built the first fur trading post at present-day Fort Pierre. It was South Dakota's first continuous white settlement (page 21).

1858 Treaty
The Sioux are forced to sign the 1858 Treaty, ceding most of present-day eastern South Dakota to the US.

1861 Dakota Territory
Congress created Dakota Territory consisting of present-day North Dakota, South Dakota, and parts of Montana and Wyoming. President James Buchanan named William Jayne of Illinois as the first governor. The capital for the territory was located in Yankton.

1862-1868 Sioux Uprising
The Minnesota Sioux almost starved to death due to the incompetence and corruption of federal agents. They were told by unsympathetic agents that they were "free to eat grass." On August 17, the Sioux Uprising, under the leadership of Chief Taoyateduta, known as Little Crow, began in Minnesota when the Sioux killed some white settlers. On August 25, a Sioux party, sent to scout out Sioux Falls, killed Judge J.B. Amidon and his son (see page 60). Within two days, Governor Jayne ordered Sioux Falls to evacuate to Yankton. The village was razed by the Sioux and sat unoccupied for three years. During the uprising, hundreds of white settlers were killed, and the Union army was called in to put down the uprising. They captured 38 Sioux men, and President Abraham Lincoln gave the order for them to be hanged on November 5, 1862 in Mankato, Minnesota. It was the largest mass-execution in US history.

1862 Homestead Act
Congress passed the Homestead Act of 1862 attracting homesteaders to the open prairies of Dakota Territory. It offered 160 acres of free land, with the condition that within five years the homesteader will have built a house on it, dug a well, plowed 10 acres, fenced it, and lived there. Beginning January 1, 1863, thousands of homesteaders moved to Dakota Territory (see page 97).

Among those filing homestead claims were Thomas and Catherine Fountain in 1878 near Flandreau (see page 31) and Charles and Caroline Ingalls in 1897 near De Smet (see page 26).

1864 Fort Sisseton
In 1864, Fort Sisseton was established in the Dakota Territory to protect the wagon trains from Sioux Indian attacks as immigrants traveled west (see page 164).

1868 Treaty
The Sioux Uprising ended with the Fort Laramie Treaty. All Dakota Territory west of the Missouri River, including the Black Hills, was granted to the Sioux and designated as the Great Sioux Reservation.

1872 Railroad
Previously, people came to Dakota Territory by covered wagon, but in 1872 the railroads reached Vermillion; in 1873 they expanded to Yankton; and by 1880 they had reached Pierre.

1874 Black Hills Gold Rush
Despite the fact that the Black Hills were granted to the Sioux by the 1868 Treaty, Colonel George Armstrong Custer led an illegal expedition into the region. Custer discovered gold on French Creek near present-day Custer, South Dakota, but the Sioux refused to grant mining rights or to cede any land in the Black Hills.

The arrival of the railroad and the discovery of gold triggered a gold rush with thousands of white prospectors and settlers trespassing into the region. When the US government failed to take steps to prevent the treaty violation, war broke out This culminated in the The Battle at Little Big Horn, in 1876, and was the most famous battle of the Indian Wars. Crazy Horse led an alliance of Sioux and Cheyenne warriers in remarkable victory over Custer and his troops.

1876 Deadwood and Lead
With the discovery of gold, the mining camps of Deadwood and Lead (pronounced *leed*) were founded. The Homestake Mine in

Lead was the largest and most productive gold mine in the Western Hemisphere (see pages 178, 181).

In 1876, Wild Bill Hickok and Calamity Jane both settled in Deadwood. Wild Bill was killed by Jack McCall while playing poker at the #10 Saloon. Seth Bullock became the sheriff of Deadwood. Preacher Smith was killed that same year. The Ingleside Cemetery was started in Deadwood. Two years later it was moved and renamed Mount Moriah Cemetery (see page 154). During this time, several other mining camps and saloons sprang up in the area, including the Moonshine Gulch Saloon in Rochford (see page 193).

1876 Jesse James
On September 7, the James-Young Gang attempted to rob the bank in Northfield, Minnesota. Outlaw brothers, Frank and Jesse James were pursued by a posse all the way to Dakota Territory. According to legend, Jesse James escaped by jumping his horse across Devil's Gulch in South Dakota (see page 38).

1880 CB&Q
In 1880, the Chicago, Burlington and Quincy Railroad Company laid down tracks to service the mines and mills between Hill City and Keystone (see page 164).

1888 L. Frank Baum
L. Frank Baum, author of *The Wonderful Wizard of Oz,* was a resident of Aberdeen from 1888 to 1891 (see page 58). In 1890, he wrote an editorial in his newspaper, *Aberdeen Saturday Pioneer,* calling for the total annihilation of the Indian race. Some say this fueled the massacre at Wounded Knee (see page 170). In 1891, he wrote a second editorial about the massacre and repeated his call for genocide.

1889 Statehood
There was a dispute between the northern and southern regions of Dakota Territory over the location of the capital in Yankton. The territory split into the modern states of North Dakota, with its capital in Bismarck, and South Dakota, with its capital in Pierre. South Dakota became the 40th US state.

1890 Ghost Dance
The Ghost Dance was a religious movement based on the visions of Wovoka (aka Jack Wilson) a Paiute shaman from Nevada. It quickly spread among the Sioux (see page 115) and caused the US government to fear a potential uprising.

1890 Sitting Bull
Mistakenly believing he was the leader of the Ghost Dance movement, federal agents arrested and killed Sitting Bull. Chief Big Foot was next on their list (see page 117).

1890 Wounded Knee
When Big Foot heard of Sitting Bull's death, he led his people south to the Pine Ridge Reservation, but they were intercepted by US troops. On December 29, at Wounded Knee Creek, the soldiers rounded up, disarmed, and killed as many as 300 Sioux, mostly women and children. Thus, officially ending the Indian Wars (see page 207).

1892 Corn Palace
The first Corn Palace was introduced in Mitchell. Each year it features a different design and draws hundreds of thousands of visitors.

1896 Bullock Hotel
The Bullock Hotel (see page 136) in Deadwood opened and is still in operation today. Seth Bullock died in hotel room 211 in 1911 (see page 120).

1903 Green Door Brothel
Deadwood's infamous Green Door Brothel (see page 146) opened and stayed in business for 77 years.

1907 Coal Mining
Coal was discovered in Firesteel (see page 94), and South Dakota's only coal mine operated from 1907 until 1969 when the mines were official shut down.

1927 Mount Rushmore
Gutzon Borglum began work carving Mount Rushmore. The job required the assistance of nearly 400 workers, many of whom are buried in Mountain View Cemetery (see page 174) in Keystone.

1927 Hotel Alex Johnson
The Hotel Alex Johnson (see page 183) in Rapid City opened.

1928 Alonzo Ward Hotel
The Alonzo Ward Hotel (see page 72) in Aberdeen opened.

1929 Potato Creek Johnny
Deadwood resident Potato Creek Johnny (see page 154) found the largest gold nugget in the Black Hills.

1931 Wall Drug
Ted and Dorothy Hustead started the Wall Drug Store.

1938 Sturgis Motorcycle Rally
The beginning of the annual Sturgis Motorcycle Rally.

1939 Badlands National Monument
The Badlands were established as Badlands National Monument; the area was redesignated "National Park" in 1978 (see page 124).

1948 Crazy Horse Memorial
Korczak Ziolkowski began work on the Crazy Horse Memorial (see page 128). When completed, it will be the largest mountain carving in the world.

1961 Bear Butte State Park
Bear Butte was established as a State Park (see page 200).

1973 Wounded Knee
There was a 71-day standoff between federal agents and militants from the American Indian Movement (see page 207).

1980 Brothels

The Green Door and other brothels in Deadwood were raided and permanently shut down (see page 146).

1989 Gambling

Although practiced openly, gambling had been illegal in Dakota Territory since 1881. In 1947, the South Dakota Attorney General began cracking down on gambling. A state ammendment in 1989 legalized limited gambling in Deadwood (see page 136).

CENTRAL SOUTH DAKOTA

Cedar Hill Cemetery

Location: Fort Pierre, Stanley County, South Dakota

Directions: From Fort Pierre take US 83, turn west on West Second. Turn right onto North Second. This road will continue uphill for approximately one mile. Turn left on Cedar Hill Road and follow the road to the cemetery.

Ghost Lore

In movies, haunted cemeteries always seem to be old, run down, and they are inevitably positioned far enough out in the country so that no one could hear you scream. But these cemeteries only exist in movies—right? Well, actually, Cedar Hill Cemetery fits the stereotypical haunted cemetery perfectly. Sitting several miles from town, the cemetery is overrun with weeds and grass, while many of the tombstones are broken or severely aged. However, the Cedar Hill Cemetery doesn't just look like a haunted cemetery, it is a haunted cemetery.

- Strange noises have been reported throughout the cemetery.

- Unexplained lights are often seen through the cemetery.

History

1894 – The land was surveyed and laid into the Union Cemetery plot by F.W. Pettigrew. During this time the maintenance of the cemetery was conducted by the lot owners.

1933 – The Union Cemetery name was changed to Cedar Hill Cemetery due to the number of cedar trees on the land.

The cemetery was so run down and dilapidated that many graves were re-interred at the Scotty Philip Cemetery.

According to the Stanley County Register of Deeds, the cemetery has 692 known graves and several unmarked graves. Many infa-

mous Stanley County residents are buried in the cemetery.

Currently — The cemetery is maintained and operated by the City of Fort Pierre.

Investigation

Many people refer to the cemetery as the "old cemetery near the Verendrye Monument." Others simply know the place as the "haunted cemetery."

The legend of the cemetery being haunted has been around for many years.

We spoke with a young lady who informed us that she had heard stories of people venturing out to the cemetery to see if it was haunted. While out at the cemetery, they would often see ghostly apparitions and hear unexplained noises.

Often those brave enough to venture out to this cemetery report seeing mysterious balls of light hovering throughout the cemetery.

Verendrye Monument

Location: Fort Pierre, Stanley County, South Dakota

Directions: Take US 83 to Fort Pierre and the monument is right off of 83.

Ghost Lore

In 1743, the Verendrye brothers told local inhabitants that they were using the plate to honor the harmony in which they shared with the native peoples. Little did the natives know that the brothers were actually claiming the land for France. Many years later, the plate was accidentally dug up by students. However, the plate may not be the only thing they dug up, as many people believe that ghostly spirits still linger in the area.

- Strange noises have been heard at the sight.

- Weird lights have been seen near the monument.

History

1743 – The Verendrye brothers, Chevalier and Louis, who were French-Canadian, buried a lead plate on the hill claiming the land for Louis XV, King of France.

1913 – The plate was accidentally discovered by several high school students.

1933 – The State Historical Society and the Fort Pierre Commercial Club erected a monument to the site that was later designated as a National Historical Landmark.

2004 – The Verendrye Monument National Historic Landmark received a $50,000 grant for monument restoration.

2005 – The monument was renovated. The first step included returning the bluff with its natural grasses, adding signs, improving

parking, and redoing the claim site marking. The second phase of the renovation overhauled the entrance road.

Currently – The seven by eight inch plate is on display in the Cultural Heritage Center in Pierre.

Investigation

Many of the residents of Fort Pierre had heard of the paranormal stories surrounding the monument, yet none of them could pinpoint where the stories began.

A man was visiting the monument when he heard unexplained noises of people talking when no one else was around.

Several visitors and those living near the monument report seeing strange balls of light that will appear and disappear with no apparent cause. These "spook lights" have been reported for several years.

IOOF Cemetery

Location: Gregory, Gregory County, South Dakota
AKA: The International Order of Odd Fellows Cemetery
Address: 47 Park Street, Gregory, SD 57533

Directions: Take Highway 18 to 47N. Turn west (left) on the first road past the football field. The cemetery will be on your right and the pavement ends there as well.

Ghost Lore

For ages, cemeteries have been known to be hotbeds of paranormal activity. Cemetery locations were once chosen because the land was thought to be a portal between the living world and the spirit world. Thus it would be much easier for your loved one to move from the living world into the spirit world. Some residents of Gregory believe that those in the IOOF cemetery may be using that portal. However, they feel that people are not going to the spirit world, they are coming from it.

- A strange man has been spotted wandering around the cemetery and gravel road.

- The man moving around the cemetery is looking for a final resting place.

History

Much of the history of the cemetery is unknown, which adds to the mysterious nature of the story. Although the exact date the cemetery was established is unknown, we do know that several of the tombstones date back to the early 1900s.

The IOOF cemetery was not the original cemetery in Gregory and the first main cemetery occupied a different location.

The cemetery is maintained by the IOOF (International Organization of Odd Fellows). The Gregory IOOF was established in 1908 and is believed to have maintained the cemetery since their inception.

Investigation

We spoke with several residents of Gregory who had heard of the story of the wandering "man," but they did not have any personal experiences.

It is a local tradition for the high school seniors to try to scare the freshman students by driving them out to the cemetery and leaving them to walk back to town on their own.

Those passing through the cemetery report seeing the ghost of a white-haired man wandering the road near the cemetery. When the man is approached, he disappears into thin air. Often, those who witness the man feel as though he is lost or is searching for something.

The Dare. The dare at the cemetery is to approach the man and ask him a question.

Bank of Midland

Location: Midland, Haakon County, South Dakota
AKA: First National Bank of Midland
Address: Main Street, Midland, SD 57552

Directions: It is on the main street of Midland.

Ghost Lore

Banks provide us with a safe, reliable, secure, and convenient place to house our money. However, this wasn't always the case as many years ago residents of the US had numerous reasons to be concerned about their life savings. From renegade bank robbers and unstoppable fires to the bank simply running out of money, townsfolk had to keep a vigilant eye on their money. Although the Midland Bank is now part of the town museum and has not been in operation for decades, many people feel that past residents are still cautiously looking after their money—even from the grave.

- Many strange things take place in the old bank in town.

- Mysterious footsteps have been heard in the bank.

- Bare footprints have been found in the bank.

History

1890 – The town of Midland was established. The town was named for its location of being halfway between the Missouri and South Fork of the Cheyenne River.

1890 – The first store was built in Midland by J. C. "Charlie" Russell.

1906 – The Bank of Midland was issued a charter.

1909 – The Bank of Midland opened. The building was constructed with Stanley County Brick and Black Hills Sandstone.

C.L. Millett was the first president of the bank. The basement of the building was used to publish the *Midland Mail*. The bank was known as the First National Bank.

1986 – The building was placed on the National Register of Historic Places.

The building is currently owned by the Midland Pioneer Museum.

Investigation

We spoke with several residents who had heard the story of the old bank being haunted, but did not have a personal experience.

The inside of the building does have a creepy feel to it as much of it is left untouched from the way it was in the past.

We did find numerous footprints in the dust of the building, yet we were unable to spot any that were barefoot.

Visitors to the museum bank report hearing strange sounds while inside the bank.

Other visitors report hearing strange noises from inside the building. The building is extremely old and in poor condition and this may account for some of the strange noises being reported.

Rock Hill

Location: Mission, Todd County, South Dakota

Directions: From Highway 18 turn right on 83. The hill will be approximately three miles on your right.

Ghost Lore

The small town of Mission is surrounded by beautiful hills and rock formations. Tucked away in the southern half of the state, the town is often overlooked as a means to get to the Black Hills. Those who stop and spend some time in Mission may find that it is stranger than it looks. Haunted areas are often believed to be sites of murders, suicides, and untimely deaths. Although this is not always the case, in Mission, the old lore may actually be true.

- A spirit of a Native American woman haunts the area.

- Unexplained noises have been reported by the old hill.

History

We struggled to find any historical information about Mission.

Just north of where the town of Mission now sits, there was an Indian encampment. The encampment housed many Native Americans before they moved to other lands.

Folklore tells of the story of Indian women and children being killed by pioneers while running for their lives.

Additional details about the deaths are unknown.

Investigation

We were unable to find any information on the slaughter of the Native American encampment that once inhabited Rock Hill.

We spoke with a gentleman who grew up in Mission and had heard stories of the ghosts of the hill since he was a child. Although he had no personal experience, he was thoroughly convinced that the spirits still roam the hill.

While driving down the old dirt road towards Rock Hill, several residents have heard ghostly screams coming from where the old encampment once was. The witnesses are baffled when, upon investigation, they can not find any source of the eerie sounds.

In addition to the ghostly screams, several witnesses have reported actually seeing the ghosts of Native Americans roaming around the old hill. They are believed to be the spirits of those killed by the pioneers, forever warning those who will listen.

Those in town call the spirits *"Wanagi,"* meaning ghost.

Most of the paranormal reports of sightings center around the rugged dirt road near the hill. It is while driving on the road that people encounter many of the apparitions and strange noises.

Many of the residents refused to speak about the spirits of Rock Hill.

Masonic Temple

Location: MItchell, Davison County, South Dakota
Address: 112 East Fifth Avenue, Mitchell, SD 57301-2632
Phone: (605) 996-4724

Ghost Lore

We have heard of places having the proverbial "skeleton in the closet," but this is the first time we have encountered a situation where it might be literally true.

Rumors are whispered of a tragic event at the Masonic Temple in Mitchell involving a young mother and her infant. People who visit the Temple sometimes report hearing the muffled sobs of a grieving woman coming from behind a closed door on the upper floor; others report the ghostly wails of a small baby. When concerned people rush to the room and open the door, the crying immediately stops when they flick on the light, but the room is empty.

It has also been reported that upon searching the rooms for the source of these mysterious sounds, some people have come face-to-face with a skeleton hanging in the closet of a nearby room.

History

The three-story Masonic Temple was built in the early 1920s and dedicated in 1924. It has been renovated in recent years and was rededicated May, 2004, on the 80th anniversary of the original ceremony.

The Temple houses two lodge rooms, a kitchen, dining room, ballroom, English Club style lounge, billiard mezzanine, and board room.

Resurgam Lodge #31, which meets in this Temple, was established in 1881 under Brothers Winslow S. Warren (Worshipful Master), H.E. Hitchcock (Senior Warden), and F. Andres (Junior Warden).

Investigation

We have been unable to find any evidence connecting the death of a mother and child to the Temple. It is unclear as to why this type of haunting activity would be encountered here.

The answer as to whether or not a skeleton hangs in one of the closets remains a secret behind closed doors.

LaFramboise Island Nature Area

Location: Pierre, Hughes County, South Dakota
Mailing Address: LaFramboise Island Nature Area, C/O Farm Island Recreation Area, 1301 Farm Island Road, Pierre, SD 57501-5829
Phone: (605) 773-2885
Email: FarmIsland@state.sd.us
Website: www.sdgfp.info/parks/Regions/OaheSharpe/ LaFramboiseIsland.htm

Directions: From Highway 14 turn west onto Popular Avenue. Follow the pier all the way back until you reach the island.

Ghost Lore

LaFramboise island sits perfectly hitched on the beautiful Missouri River, just outside the bustling city of Pierre. The island is approximately three miles long and nearly one mile wide. Heavily forested with cottonwood trees, meadows, and a variety of birds and other wildlife, LaFramboise allows visitors to hike, bike, or walk with the added benefit of finding some solitude. However, those spending time relaxing on the island that was dubbed "Bad Humor" by explorers Lewis and Clark may find that they are not alone at all.

- Extreme temperature changes are felt in certain spots of the trails.

- Hikers hear strange noises coming from the island.

- Investigators have captured strange balls of light (orbs) on film.

History

1804 – Lewis and Clark passed through the area checking out the island.

1811 – Several fur traders passed by the island.

1817 – Joseph LaFramboise constructed the first post located at Fort Pierre. This Fort was credited as being the first continuous white settlement in South Dakota.

1822 – Fort LaFramboise was replaced by Fort Tecumseh.

1855 – The US Army purchased Fort Pierre for $45,000.

1856 – LaFramboise passed away.

1857 – Fort Pierre was torn down and abandoned.

1890s – The island appeared on a map drawn up by the US Army Corps of Engineers.

1893 – The island was divided into three parcels owned by citizens.

1950s – The island was used for farming.

1962 – The US Army Corps of Engineers purchased the island.

1979 – The US Army Corps of Engineers designated the island as a natural area.

2002 – LaFramboise Island's fee title was transferred from the US Army Corps of Engineers to the State of South Dakota.

2004 – Over 20,000 visits were made to the island.

Investigation

Lewis and Clark dubbed the island "Bad Humor Island" due to their tense encounter with the nearby Teton Sioux.

The island is currently named after Joseph LaFramboise.

While on the island, visitors will encounter cold chills as they experience an unexplainable temperature drop. However, the cold spot often dissipates just as quickly as it formed.

Often times visitors will be walking through the island when they hear strange noises coming from the trees. Many believe that the noises are caused by the spirit of former Native Americans who lived in the area.

It has been reported that several investigators have caught strange balls of lights (orbs) on their film while on the island.

(Additional Research provided by the South Dakota Department of Game, Fish and Parks.)

EASTERN SOUTH DAKOTA

Ingalls

Location: De Smet, Kingsbury County, South Dakota

Ingalls Homestead
Address: 20812 Homestead Road, De Smet, SD 57231-5841
Phone: 1-800-776-3594
Website: www.ingallshomestead.com
Directions: From De Smet, drive one-half mile southeast on Hwy 14 to Homestead Road. Go south three-quarters of a mile. Enter at top of hill through Visitor Center.

De Smet Cemetery
Directions: From De Smet, drive one-half mile south on Hwy 25. Turn right on 208th St. Cemetery is another one-half mile on the left.

Ghost Lore

Most of us are familiar with *The Little House on the Prairie* television series and the books written by Laura Ingalls Wilder, but some would suggest a book could be written entitled *The Haunted Little House on the Prairie.*

The Ingalls Homestead in De Smet is still standing and open to the public for tours. Many visitors believe the spirits of Pa and Ma Ingalls still reside in the home where they raised their children. Intuitive people have sensed the lingering presence of the famous parents and encountered cold spots and moving shadows. Some tourists report hearing hushed voices coming from empty rooms.

The De Smet Cemetery, where Pa and Ma Ingalls are buried, is also rumored to be haunted. Shadowy figures have been seen in the cemetery at night. The most commonly reported phenomenon is a mysterious faint light known as a will-o'-the-wisp. This luminous orb will appear late at night and dart between trees and gravestones, only to disappear when the curious venture too closely.

History

1836 – Charles "Pa" Philip Ingalls was born.

1839 – Caroline "Ma" Lake Quiner Ingalls was born.

1857 – February 13. Almanzo James Wilder was born to James and Angeline Day Wilder near Malone, New York.

1860 – Charles and Caroline were married.

1867 – February 7. Laura Elizabeth Ingalls was born to Charles and Caroline at the edge of the "Big Woods" in a log cabin near Pepin, Wisconsin. Laura was the second of five children. Her siblings were Mary Amelia (who later became blind), Caroline Celestia (known as Carrie), Charles Frederic (known as Freddy, died at age one), and Grace Pearl.

1869 – The Ingalls family moved extensively throughout the Midwest living in a covered wagon, a dugout, a log cabin, and various shanties.

1879 – Charles filed a homestead claim near De Smet in the Dakota Territory and moved the family there for good.

1882 – Laura received her first teaching certificate.

1885 – August 25. Laura and Almanzo were married by the Reverend E. Brown of the Congregational Church and made their home in De Smet.

1886 – Rose Wilder was born to Laura and Almanzo.

1888-1889 – A series of tragedies struck. Almanzo and Laura contracted diphtheria. Almanzo suffered a stroke that left him partially paralyzed and permanently crippled. They lost their house to fire.

1889 – Laura and Almanzo had a baby boy who was born on Aug.12th and died on Aug. 24th, 1889. He was buried in De Smet Cemetery.

1902 – Pa Ingalls died and was buried in the De Smet cemetery.

1924 – Ma Ingalls died and was buried in the De Smet cemetery.

1928 – Mary Ingalls died and was buried in the De Smet cemetery.

1932 – *Little House in the Big Woods* was published.

1933 – *Farmer Boy* was published.

1935 – *Little House on the Prairie* was published.

1937 – *On the Banks of Plum Creek* was published.

1939 – *By the Shores of Silver Lake* was published.

1940 – *The Long Winter* was published.

1941 – Grace died and was buried in the De Smet cemetery. *Little*

Town on the Prairie was published.

1943 – *These Happy Golden Years* was published.

1946 – Carrie died and was buried in the De Smet cemetery.

1949 – Almanzo died.

1957 – Laura died.

1962 – *On the Way Home* was published.

1971 – *The First Four Years* was published.

Laura wrote five books that described her life in De Smet: *By the Shores of Silver Lake, The Long Winter, Little Town on the Prairie, These Happy Golden Years,* and *The First Four Years.*

Investigation

Ingalls Homestead. The house on the homestead is actually a reconstruction, but it is built to the original dimensions and on the original spot. The accurary of the construction is verified by the homestead patent at the National Archives in Washington DC. Some of the trees on the property are also the original trees planted by the Ingalls.

Would spirits haunt a reconstruction or are they only attached to the original structures? It's hard to say. Perhaps they have an affinity for the land itself.

De Smet Cemetery. Laura and her husband Almanzo are buried in Mansfield, Missouri, but the graves of Laura's son, parents, and three sisters can be found in the De Smet Cemetery. The family plot is found on block 44, lot 9. Whether or not the haunting activity in the cemetery is caused by any of the Ingalls is indeterminate.

Ingalls Family Buried in
De Smet Cemetery

Baby Boy Wilder
b. August 12, 1889
d. August 24, 1889
Son of Almanzo and Laura Ingalls Wilder.

Charles Philip Ingalls
b. January 10, 1836
d. June 8, 1902
Father of Laura Ingalls Wilder.

Caroline Lake Quiner Ingalls
b. December 12, 1839
d. April 20, 1924
Mother of Laura Ingalls Wilder.

Mary Amelia Ingalls
b. January 10, 1865
d. October 17, 1928
Sister of Laura Ingalls Wilder.

Grace Pearl Dow (Ingalls)
b. May 23, 1877
d. November 10, 1941
Sister of Laura Ingalls Wilder. She married Nathan
William Dow in 1901.

Caroline Celestia Ingalls Swanzey
b. August 3, 1870
d. June 2, 1946
Sister of Laura Ingalls Wilder.

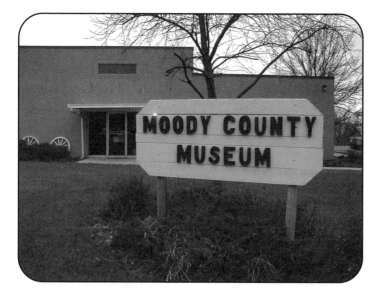

Moody County Museum

Location: Flandreau, Moody County, South Dakota
Mailing Address: P.O. Box 25, Flandreau, SD 57028-0025
Street Address: 706 East Pipestone Avenue, Flandreau, SD 57028
Phone: (605) 997-2786 (For tour or appointment) or (605) 997-3191

Ghost Lore

They say we spend one-third of our entire life sleeping, so it is not surprising that we become emotionally attached to our beds. But does that attachment end at death or can beds become haunted? We have heard the expression, "waking the dead," but where do the dead sleep? In the graveyard? Or do they sometimes choose to spend their eternal rest in a more comfortable place, by seeking out the beds that used to belong to them? This is the question being asked at the Moody County Museum, where a bed almost 130 years old is on display. The story is that the previous owner of the bed returns each night after-hours to make certain her property is being appropriately cared for. She reclines on her bed and sleeps until sunrise, then vanishes as the ephemeral morning dew disappears.

History of the Museum

1964 – The museum was constructed.

1965 – July 4. Grand opening of the newly-built Moody County Museum. It contained a collection of early pioneer and American Indian artifacts from Moody County.

1966 – The bedroom set was donated to the museum by Mr. and Mrs. Claude Krech.

Allie Fountain's haunted bed

History of the Bed

1865 – Feb 16. Thomas James Fountain Jr. was born in Denver, Iowa, to Thomas Fountain Sr. and Catherine Margaret (nee Barclay) Fountain. As a young boy he was forever singing "Pat McGuire" (aka "Pat Maguire"), a popular ballad at that time. Consequently, he was given the nickname of "Pat," which stuck with him for the rest of his life.

1871 – July 12. Alma Asenath Lee was born in Orchard, Iowa, to Julius Anson Lee and Susannah Mariah (nee King) Lee. She was known to the family as "Allie."

1878 – Thomas and Catherine realized that because of the high price of land in Iowa, their children would never be able to own their own property, so they decided to move the family to Dakota Territory. Pat, the youngest child, was only thirteen years old at the time. They sold their home, loaded up their covered wagons, and

The haunted mannequin.

set off in an oxen-driven wagon train that included Pat's three older, married sisters: Celecta "Lecky" and husband Manuel Winklepleck; Frances "Franky" and husband Charley Dyce; and Evalina "Lina" and husband William Krech. They settled near the town of Colman in Moody County.

It was at this time that a large, solid, maple bed was shipped to Pat from White Pigeon, Michigan. The Fountain family was originally from Yorkshire, England and had settled in White Pigeon in 1848, so it is possible the bed was sent by his grandparents or other relatives who may have still been living there at the time.

1884 – March 28. Pat's nephew, Claude Eugene Krech, was born to Lina and William Krech in Colman.

1886 – Pat and Allie first met.

1893 – January 27. Pat (age 27) and Allie (age 21) were married in

The orange metal doors.

Jefferson Twp., Moody Co., South Dakota, after what Allie referred to as a "seven-year engagement." They moved in with Pat's parents near Colman and helped care for his ailing mother, Catherine, who was paralyzed by a stroke.

1894 – January 15. Pat & Allie's daughter Ina May Fountain was born.

1896 – November 22. Pat & Allie's daughter Cecile Fountain was born. Pat"s mother Catherine died at the age of 73 and was buried in Mount Auburn Cemetery.

1900 – Pat and Allie had a son, Glenn Eugene, who was born February 17 but died October 26. He was buried in Mount Auburn Cemetery.

1902 – Pat moved from his parent's farm after building his own farm across the road. He also built a general store.

1903 – Pat's father Thomas died at the age of 76 and was buried in Mount Auburn Cemetery.

1910 – March 12. Pat & Allie's daughter Viva Faye Fountain was born.

1911 – Pat sold his house and the store and moved his family to Flandreau. Eventually the three daughters married and started families of their own. Ina married Clarence E. Peterson; Cecile married J. Arthur Whaley; and Viva Faye married William Kelly.

1914 – Both Allie's parents died.

1920 – October. Pat died at the age of 56 and was buried in Mount Auburn Cemetery in Moody.

1950 – Allie may have been living with one of her daughters in Asotin, Washington, when she died December 27th, at the age of 79. She was buried in Mount Auburn Cemetery next to her beloved husband Pat.

1966 – The bed that belonged to Pat and Allie had been passed down to Pat's nephew Claude E. Krech. Eighty-two-year-old Claude and his wife Eva Myrtle donated the bed to the Moody County Museum.

Investigation

The curator and employees report that after the bed was donated to the museum, strange things began to happen. Initially, they would catch glimpses of movement in their peripheral vision. Sometimes plaques would mysteriously tip over. But things got progressively stranger. Two orange, metal doors, that were extremely heavy, would open and slam shut on their own. No logical explanation could be found. The floors were level, and because of the size and weight of the doors, it took a great deal of exertion to even move them. One of the employees who first witnessed this event was so terrified, she resigned that very day.

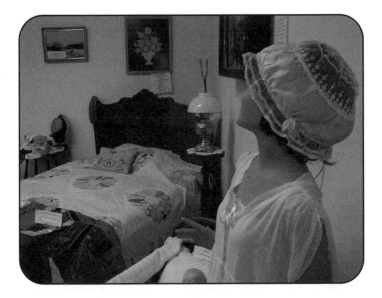

The mannequin stands next to the bed

Most of the activity was occurring near the bed on display, and employees became suspicious that there was a connection. Their suspicions were confirmed when they came in early one morning and discovered a mannequin positioned near the bed was missing its blond wig. The wig was found on the floor near the mannequin, but there was no explanation as to how it could have been lifted up off the head and tossed onto the floor. There were no air vents above or near the display, and the employees were certain nothing had been disturbed the previous night when they closed up. This time the employees made doubly certain that the wig was secured to the mannequin's head before closing up, but the next morning they were shocked to find the wig once again on the floor. By this point, they were convinced the museum was haunted and began referring to the ghost as "Sarah." Because of her behavior with the wig, they assumed Sarah had a dislike of blonds.

A few days later, an employee noticed a depression on the bed, as if somebody had been sitting on the quilt. The bed was roped off, and patrons were not allowed to touch the bed, much less to sit on it, so it seemed strange that this sunken impression would be found on the mattress. The quilt was straightened, but the next morning the employees returned to once again find an indentation on the bedding as if somebody had been sitting or laying there overnight. This became a regular event.

Convinced the bed was the source of the haunting activity, the curator and employees decided to research its history, and that was when they learned it had belonged to Pat and Allie Fountain. From that point on, they began to refer to the ghost as "Allie," and this seemed to appease the spirit and much of the haunting activity has abated. However, many people still believe that Allie remains in the museum, keeping a vigilant watch over her furniture and eternally sleeping in the comfort of her own bed.

Devil's Gulch

Location: Garretson, Minnehaha County, South Dakota
Mailing Address: Devil's Gulch, Town of Garretson, P.O. Box 370, Garretson, SD 57030
Phone: (605) 594-6721
Email: kvegas@splitrocktel.net

Directions: Garretson is located about 20 miles northeast of Sioux Falls. From exit 406 on I-90, take Cty. Rd. 11 to Garretson. Turn east at sign for Devil's Gulch.

Ghost Lore

A wooden sign here reads, "Welcome to Devil's Gulch. Home of beauty, mystery, and legend." Indeed, you can expect precisely that. Many tourists have reported unexplained sights and sounds in this place of legends. Although at most places haunting activity occurs after dark, here it can be experienced during daylight.

- White vaporous apparitions have been seen floating under the footbridge.

- Strange moaning sounds have been heard coming from deep within the gulch and in various other locations.

- Voices have been heard coming from the forest.

The Legend of Iktomi. Among the Lakota people, stories are told of Iktomi, a spirit whom they admired for his courage and wisdom. At one time there was a warrior named Ha-Shootch-Ga who was instigating trouble by going around to all the tribes and starting rumors to cause them to mistrust each other. This culminated in a confrontation between Ha-Shootch-Ga and Iktomi near the Split Rock River. The warrior uttered threats and insults to Iktomi, then challenged him to a duel with tomahawks to see who was the greatest warrior. As the two engaged in a stare down, Ha-Shootch-Ga could see flames of fire in the eyes of Iktomi. This terrified

Gulch jumped by Jesse James.

him, and he quickly turned and ran away. Iktomi threw his mighty tomahawk at the heels of the retreating warrior, striking the earth with such an explosive force that it split the rocky ground and formed the canyon known today as the Devil's Gulch. To this day, the spirit of Iktomi still resides in the canyon.

The Legend of Nellie Harding. This young woman was traveling by covered wagon with her parents and brother through Dakota Territory when they were attacked by a small party of Indians near the Sioux River. The Indians, led by a white outlaw, abducted the girl and killed her family. Meanwhile, back in Wisconsin, her boyfriend, Dick Willowby, had a clairvoyant dream that showed him what had happened and where to find her. He immediately set out on horseback with the intentions of rescuing her.

Dick found them hiding in the Devil's Gulch, and a shootout ensued, resulting in the death of all the Indians. As the outlaw was using Nellie as a human shield, Dick fired a shot intended for the outlaw, but instead accidentally killed his lover.

With a vengeful anger, Dick pursued the outlaw on horseback for over five miles. The gun battle continued, and Dick was shot and mortally wounded. It looked as if the outlaw would make a clean get away, until his horse stumbled on the rocky terrain, and the outlaw hit his head and died instantly. Dick Willowby, weak from a loss of blood, managed to get himself back to the body of his beloved Nellie Harding and died while holding her in his arms. Many believe the spirits of the two lovers haunt the canyon.

The Legend of Jesse James. After the famous Northfield bank robbery, a posse of over 500 men pursued the James-Younger Gang. The James brothers split up from the rest of the gang and headed for Dakota Territory. When they came to Split Rock River, Jesse James went on the east side and his brother Frank rode on the west side. A posse picked up Jesse's trail and chased him as far as Devil's Gulch and had him cornered. The only thing that stood between the outlaw and freedom was a 20-foot expanse across the river. As the posse closed in on him, Jesse decided to go for broke.

He spurred his horse and made a daring leap over the canyon, landing safely on the other side. His pursuers were so amazed at his miraculous feat, they abandoned the chase. On the other side, Jesse met up with Frank. They hid out in a small cave in the bluffs for a couple of days, then safely rode back to Missouri. It is said Devil's Gulch is haunted by the ghost of Jesse James.

Legend of the Devil. Despite the natural beauty of this area, some people have the notion that the Devil haunts this place and wanders the grounds at night. Besides the Devil's Gulch, you can also visit formations named the Devil's Stairway and Devil's Kitchen. Supposedly a sinister presence is felt here.

History

Jesse James. On September 5, 1847, Jesse Woodson James was born to Robert and Zerelda James in Centerville, Missouri. His father was a slave-owning Baptist minister who farmed hemp and tobacco. In 1863, Jesse's older brother Frank joined the Confederate Bushwhackers. The following year, 16-year-old Jesse also joined up. After the Civil War, the brothers became outlaws, eventually teaming up with fellow Bushwhackers Cole, Jim, and Bob Younger. The legendary James-Younger Gang robbed trains, banks, and stagecoaches throughout Arkansas, Iowa, Kansas, Kentucky, Missouri, and West Virginia.

On September 7, 1876, at 2:00 p.m., the James-Young Gang attempted to rob the bank in Northfield, Minnesota. The gang also included Charlie Pitts, Clell Miller, and William Stiles. Earlier that month, they had taken a train to Saint Paul, purchased horses, and scouted out the surrounding terrain. By this time, they were the most famous gang of outlaws in the nation, and after a series of successful robberies, they expected the Northfield bank to be an easy job; however, things did not quite go as planned.

They split up into three groups: those who actually robbed the bank (Frank James, Bob Younger, and Charlie Pitts), those who guarded the bank entrance (Cole Younger and Clell Miller), and those who secured the escape route (Jesse James, Jim Younger, and William Stiles).

Joseph Lee Heywood, the head teller of the bank, was shot and killed after refusing to open the safe. When it became obvious that their bank was being heldup, the local citizens sent up the alarm and went after their guns. The outlaws fired a few warning shots in the air to clear the streets for their getaway, but the townspeople started shooting back from undercover. William Stiles and Clell Miller were killed. Nicholas Gustafson, an innocent bystander on the street, was hit by a stray bullet and also killed.

The surviving gang members fled empty-handed, but a posse of hundreds of men was rounded up and tracked them through southwestern Minnesota. By the time the gang reached Elysian, Minnesota, their horses were exhausted, so they abandoned them and continued on foot. When they were spotted near Mankato, they decided it would be best to split up. The James brothers stole some horses and headed south, while the three Younger brothers and Charlie Pitts continued west on foot. While camping near Minneopa, the Youngers and Pitts were again spotted. During a shootout, Pitts was killed, and the badly wounded Youngers were captured. Bob Younger was shot in the chest; earlier he had been shot in the elbow. Also, part of Jim Younger's jaw was shot off, and he was never to eat solid food again.

Frank and Jesse did make it as far as Dakota Territory and later back to Missouri without being captured by the posse.

Investigation

The Devil's Gulch has been preserved as a municipal park by the city of Garretson. It is open to the public and guided tours are available. A steel footbridge has been constructed over the expanse where Jesse James allegedly made his jump.

The river is walled by beautiful Sioux quartzite palisades, and the dark waters below are incredibly deep--some even say bottomless.

Investigators took plumb line readings to determine its depth and gave up after dropping 600 feet of line.

A trail leads to the "Jesse James Cave," on Split Rock River where Jesse and Frank allegedly holed up, waiting for the posse to leave. It's on private property and not open to the public. Apparently Jesse carved his name in the quartzite stone wall of the cave.

Although many legends surround Jesse James, much of the Northfield bank robbery is well-documented historically. Jesse's leap over Devil's Gulch is, however, questionable. Some people doubt that a horse could jump that far. Others wonder why the posse did not just go around the gulch and continue their pursuit since they were so close to capturing him.

It seems strange that the ghost of Jesse James would haunt Devil's Gulch, considering the fact he died six years later and over 300 miles south of this location. Jesse James was assassinated by his friends, the Ford Brothers, on April 3, 1882 at Saint Joseph, Missouri. He had taken off his guns and was standing on a chair to dust a picture when they drew their guns and shot him.

Most people we spoke with doubted that the gulch was haunted by the devil. They reported feeling a sense of mystery and awe, but nothing suggested an evil presence here.

We could find no historical information to verify the story of Dick Willowby and Nellie Harding. It could be nothing more than a legend.

For centuries the Native Americans have believed spirits dwelled in this area and referred to it as Spirit Canyon. Perhaps these are the same spirits tourists have encounted.

Abandoned Building

Location: Iroquois, Kingsbury County, South Dakota

Directions: Corner of Quapaw Street and Washita. Next to Lazy "R" Bar. From Highway 14 turn south on Quapaw. The building will be on the corner of Quapaw and Washita Street.

Ghost Lore

Looking at this historic building, one is easily swept away to the time when the boarded up building was bustling with life. Many people travel to this rural town during pheasant hunting season. Most hunters probably do not even notice the old boarded-up building on the corner of the crossroads. However, locals have been doing their own hunting at the building—hunting for ghosts, that is.

- The building was once a mortuary.

- A stray coffin still lingers in the building.

- Curtains are mysteriously drawn back on their own.

- Windows seem to fog over for no apparent reason.

History

1884 – The building was constructed as the Farmers and Merchants Bank.

1886 – The F & M Bank was incorporated.

1890s – Many businesses moved in and out of the building including a hardware store and real estate offices.

The upper portion of the building was used for apartments.

The last business in the building was the Hoevet Funeral Home.

The building has been closed for over 25 years.

The South Dakota Historical Society was contacted about assisting with saving the building. However, the status of the request is unknown.

Investigation

The building was a mortuary that housed the Hoevet Funeral Home.

For Halloween 2004, the community used the building for a haunted house. Apparently the organizers did not remove the props as they had promised. These left over props may explain the coffin that is often spotted in the building.

We spoke with a shop keeper who informed us that she had heard stories of people seeing weird lights moving through the building when it was suppoedly vacant.

Many residents believe that the ghosts are the spirits of those who where brought in when the building was the Hoevet Funeral Home.

A bartender who works next door at the Lazy "R" Bar told us that although she had heard numerous people talk of ghosts in the building, she had no personal experiences. She also reported that stray cats often get into the building and may account for some of the strange noises.

Those who lived in the building while it was being used for apartments reported hearing the bizarre sounds of things moving around, yet the source of the noise was never found.

A former resident of the building reported hearing odd noises that could not be accounted for.

Another couple also had a bizarre experience while living in the apartment. One summer night a man came home to find his wife in bed. The husband immediately noticed that his wife looked terrified and was holding a gun in her hands and seemed visibly shaken. When the man asked his wife if she was okay, she informed her husband that the gun was meant to protect herself from the ghosts in the apartment.

The Lamp Post Inn

Location: Madison, Lake County, South Dakota
Official Name: The Lamp Post Inn Bed & Breakfast
Address: 621 North Washington Avenue, Madison, SD 57042-1633
Phone: (605) 427-0324
Cell Phone: (605) 270-9529
Email: lamppost@iw.net
Website: www.bbonline.com/sd/lamppost
Innkeepers: John & Linda Wagner

Directions: Madison is located 45 miles NW of Sioux Falls.

Ghost Lore

In 1884, Sarah Winchester, heir to the fortune of the Winchester Rifle company, moved to California and began spending her $20 million inheritance on the construction of what came to be known as the Winchester Mystery House. Believing the Winchester family was cursed by the spirits of all the people who had been killed by the Winchester rifle, the wealthy widow built the house with bizarre features in hopes of attracting good spirits and repelling bad spirits. There were hallways and doors that lead nowhere, secret passages and stairways, and curved walls. She also built several fireplaces, believing the vengeful spirits would use them as an exit.

Fifteen years later, and long before the popularity of Feng-shui, a similar house was built in Madison utilizing some of the same principles. Although not as extravagant or outlandish as the Winchester Mystery House, it does incorporate some unusually shaped rooms, curved walls, and a fireplace with a quarter-sawn oak mantelpiece.

The home currently operates as a popular bed-and-breakfast, and many people attribute the safe and comfortable atmosphere it exudes to the unique layout of the house.

It is believed the design of the house keeps away malicious spooks, but attracts friendly ghosts, including the gentle and caring spirit of J.R. Westaby, a country doctor who once lived here.

History of the House

1899 – Prof. Joel W. and Frances Shaw Goff built a two-story house on the lot they purchased from Charles B. Kennedy.

1927 – March. The property was sold to Dr. J.R. and Marcia B. Westaby. Mrs. Westaby enjoyed a beautiful yard and goldfish pond. Dr. Westaby later enclosed the southern part of the porch so his ailing wife could sit outside.

1970 – Dr. Westaby donated the house to the Dakota State College scholarship fund.

1984 – August. Robert and Char Haar purchased the house.

1987 – The Haars remodeled the house.

The Goff House

1995 – Alan & Julie Gross purchased the house.

2005 – February. John & Linda Wagner bought the house and converted it into a bed-and-breakfast.

History of the Westabys

1883 – Spencer George and Mary Eleanor Westaby moved from Illinois to Madison, South Dakota, and bought a homestead five miles southwest of the town.

1884 – March 24. Marcia Blanche Eldred was born in North Pownal, VT.

1885 – March 1. J.R. (John Roy) Westaby, was born to Spencer and Mary Westaby in a dugout in a creek bank near a grove.

Photo Courtesy of John & Linda Wagner.

The Westaby House

1903 – J.R. attended Coe College in Cedar Rapids, IA.

1909 – J.R. graduated with a degree in chemistry, then entered medical school at the University of Chicago Rush Medical Center.

1913 – J.R. graduated with a medical degree and worked in Chicago and Albany, NY.

1914 – December 17. J.R. married Marcia Eldred, a graduate nurse who was working as the superintendent of surgical nurses at the same Albany hospital.

1915 – J.R. moved back to South Dakota with his new bride and acquired his state medical license. He practiced medicine in Clark, SD.

Dr. Westaby
1885-1975

1919 – Dr. Westaby and his wife moved to Madison and helped his brother, Dr. R.H. Westaby, build a hospital.

1927 – Dr. Westaby purchased the house at 621 North Washington Avenue.

1930-31 – Dr. Westaby organized the Third District Medical Society. He was also the vice-president and later president of the state medical association.

1954 – August 16. Dr. Westaby's wife Marcia passed away.

1975 – June.   Dr. Westaby died at the age of 90.

Investigation

Rumors have circulated about the house being haunted. The current owners were told that the rounded walls and unique rooms were apparently designed to confuse and drive off unwanted ghosts. Whether this was a part of the original construction or the remodeling later done by the Haar family is unknown.

Dr. Westaby did practice medicine from his home, so it is possible terminally ill patients died there. Could these be the spirits people were trying to chase away?

Other people believe the kindly doctor still resides in the familiar home he loved so much. One of bedrooms in the bed-and-breakfast, with the curved walls, is believed to have been the doctor's office. It is said his presence is still felt and his footsteps are sometimes heard.

The Actor's Studio

Location: Sioux Falls, Minnehaha County, South Dakota
Address: 305 North Phillips Avenue, Sioux Falls, SD 57104-6005

Ghost Lore

People claim the Actor's Studio is haunted. Do they know what they are talking about? Or are they just . . . whistling in the dark?

Speaking of "whistling in the dark," some say this is, in fact, what the ghost literally does. Late at night, in the shadowy corners of the building, the specter can be heard shuffling across the floor and whistling the familiar tune of "Twinkle, Twinkle, Little Star."

The story we heard most often was that a young man was having an affair with an attractive woman while her fiancé (in other versions, her husband) was off to war. The soldier came home unexpectantly and caught the two lovers in a romantic embrace on the dance floor at the Rainbow Bar. The young man was the victim of a crime of passion; killed by the soldier right before the terrified eyes of the young woman. To this day, the dead man wanders the former bar looking for his former lover and whistling a child's song that apparently had some personal meaning to him.

History

It is not known when this building was first constructed, but at one time it operated as the Rainbow Bar & Grill and later as the Lime Lite Casino.

1994 – The Community Playhouse, which owned the Orpheum Theater next door, purchased the Lime Lite to use as an actor's studio. They constructed an addition, known as the "Link," to connect the two facilities.

2000 – Due to financial difficulties, the Community Playhouse was unable to keep up their payments, and the city took ownership of the building and used it as storage for the Sioux Falls Parks and Recreation Department.

2002 – The city also took possesion of the Orpheum Theater and the Link and began renovating all three buildings.

After the remodeling, the first floor of the Actor's Studio will consist of rooms for classes, rehearsals, performances, and rentals. The second floor will house the Channel 16 TV offices and studio.

The Link is being rebuilt to serve as a lobby connecting the two buildings. It will contain the box office area and restrooms.

Investigation

We are still searching for documentation to verify that a murder took place in this building. The continued haunting activity is still attested by eyewitnesses.

Orpheum Theatre

Location: Sioux Falls, Minnehaha County, South Dakota
Formerly the Sioux Falls Community Playhouse (closed in 2002)
Address: 315 North Phillips Avenue, Sioux Falls, SD 57104-6005
Phone: (605) 367-4616 (Box Office)

Ghost Lore

Theaters can excite strong emotions in people. Whether it is a concert, a play, a movie, or some other form of entertainment, it moves us and leaves a lasting impression. With so much emotive energy concentrated under one roof, it is not surprising so many playhouses are reported to be haunted.

Case in point, the historic Orpheum Theater—long rumored to be haunted by a ghost known only as "Larry."

- Feelings of being watched.

- Toilets flush on their own.

- Faucets will turn on by themselves.

- Sound of phantom footsteps.

History

1913 – October 2. The Orpheum Theater, a Beaux-Arts style vaudeville house, had its grand opening. Tickets were $5 per seat, and the first night's performance consisted of a concert by the Orpheum Orchestra, four vaudeville acts, screen projections of Pathe News, and short subjects from the Orthoscope. The 1,000-seat theater was built by brothers John and Frank Solari. The theater was connected with the Orpheum Circuit, Inc., an association of 45 theaters in 36 cities in which plays, acts, and films moved from theater to theater for presentation. Stock theater also became popular at the Orpheum.

1927 – The theater was temporarily closed and sold to a competitor.

1954 – The Community Playhouse purchased the Orpheum.

1983 – It was listed on the National Register of Historic Places.

2002 – The Sioux Falls Community Playhouse folded after 72 seasons, and the theater was purchased by the city. Over $1 million of renovation work was started on the building. An old apartment on the second floor was remodeled and used for the city's Municipal Band offices.

Investigation

When the Sioux Falls Community Playhouse first purchased the theater, they discovered an old casket down in the boiler room. They assumed the beautifully decorated coffin was formerly used as a magician's prop. Later when they returned to clean the basement, the coffin had mysteriously vanished.

In October of 1959, an actor named Ray Loftesness was alone in the theater doing a walk-through rehearsal on stage when a bright blue-green, pulsating light coming from the balcony suddenly caught his attention. Within the aura of light he could discern the figure of a man who appeared to be pointing towards him. At that very moment the actor was struck in the face by a blast of icy cold air and decided to make a hasty retreat out the back door. This was just the beginning of a series of strange events.

The next morning, stagehands arrived at the theater and found all the fuses had been mysteriously blown. During the dress rehearsal and on the opening night of their performance, a sandbag fell from the rafters hitting Ray on the head and knocking him unconscious both times.

In 1972, a technical director by the name of Jack Mortenson, vice president of the Playhouse board, was alone in the theater late at night sweeping and cleaning the stage when he discovered an old-fashioned ferrotype photo on the floor in a spot where he had just swept moments earlier. He estimated the picture dated back to about 1890, and the image was of a bearded man, probably in his 30s, with rosy cheeks and piercing eyes. A chill ran up Jack's spine, and he ran out of the building. The next day he showed it to the performers and stagehands, but nobody had ever seen it before. Most people speculated that the man in the portrait was the ghost who haunted the theater and, at that time, somebody facetiously dubbed him "Larry," a name which has stuck. The picture sat on the lightboard for several months, then one day it disappeared just as mysteriously as it had appeared.

Drama teacher Dale Hart asserts he does not believe in ghosts, yet he admits he is unable to explain the mysterious shadow of a man that appears in a photo he took of the theater's balcony. There was nobody in the balcony at the time, but the silhouette of a human figure was unquestionably cast on the wall.

Several theories have been advanced as to the identity of Larry:

- He was a former maintenance man who hanged himself in the rafters above the stage.

- He was one of the construction workers who built the theater and was killed in a work-related accident.

- He was a stagehand who was murdered backstage during a vaudeville performance.

- He was a patron of the theater, carrying-on with a married woman and was shot to death in the balcony by her angry husband.

- He was an actor, distraught over not getting the part of Romeo. During the dress rehearsal, a gun shot was heard in the light booth. Upon inspection, the actors discovered a puddle of blood, but, strangely, Larry's body was never found.

The Pioneer Memorial

Location: Sioux Falls, Minnehaha County, South Dakota

Directions: Near the intersection of US 77 and North Cliff Avenue, on the hilltop overlooking Sioux Falls.

Ghost Lore

Many people believe that spirits return from the dead to haunt a particular location because they want to be remembered, and they do not want people to forget how they died.

During the Sioux Uprising of 1862, Judge J. B. Amidon and his teenage son were killed by Indians and buried at this overlook. Ever since that day, the ghosts of the judge and his son have lingered on this hilltop to keep their memory alive and to keep a vigilant watch over the city. From a distance, people have seen mysterious spook lights--luminous orbs--that hover above the hill and move about. While standing on this spot, many report the sensation of being watched and sense a preternatural presence that seems to permeate the entire area. Late at night, some people have reportedly seen apparitions of the judge and his son ambling about on the hill. The ghostly figures still bear the marks of how they died. A bullet hole can clearly be seen in the the father's back, and the son is riddled with arrows protruding from his body.

The citizens of Sioux Falls believed the judge and his son were haunting the hilltop because they did not want to be forgotten, so the city erected this obelisk as a memorial to them.

History

Joseph Bonaparte Amidon was born in Connecticut in 1801. He lived in Saint Paul, Minnesota for a while, then moved to Sioux Falls with his wife Mahala, son William (Willie), and daughter Eliza (Lizzie), sometime before 1860.

He was a County Probate Judge, Treasurer, and Commisioner

appointed by Territorial Governor William A. Jayne and the Territorial Legislature.

During the 1862 Sioux Uprising, Chief Little Crow ordered the warrior White Lodge to drive the white settlers from the Sioux Valley. In the early morning hours of August 25, 1862, Judge J. B. Amidon and his teenage son Willie set out for their claim one mile north of their Sioux Falls cabin when they accidentally came upon White Lodge's scouting party. The judge was killed instantly by a single gun shot; his son was shot with arrows.

That evening, when they failed to return, the judge's wife became concerned and contacted the Dakota calvalry detachment stationed in Sioux Falls. The soldiers found the judge's team of yoked oxen, still hitched to the wagon, but there was no sign of the two men. The next morning, the searchers found the bodies. Amidon was laying facedown in a cornfield with a single bullet hole in his back. His son's body, found in an adjacent field, was riddled with arrows like a pin cushion full of pins. There were indications that the boy had survived long enough to pull out some of the arrows from his body.

Two days later, Governor Jayne ordered the evacuation of Sioux Falls. After the residents quickly retreated to Yankton, the Indians razed the village and Sioux Falls remained abandoned for the next three years.

Investigation

Judge Amidon and his son were not killed on this hilltop. The cornfield where they died is located where the penitentiary is now.

For a long time it was believed they were buried near a mound of boulders about 900 feet northwest of the monument, but in 1989 an archeological excavation of the site determined there was no evidence of any unmarked graves. Later that year, a second excavation with a backhoe confirmed that no bodies where buried here. There is some historical evidence that a solider, George B. Trumbo, brought their bodies back to the village of Sioux Falls and Sgt. Jesse Buel Watson buried them in a cemetery there. Some speculate that it might have been in Mount Pleasant cemetery, but the exact location of their burial remains an unsolved mystery.

The Sioux Quartzie obelisk was erected in 1949, but it was not the result of the alleged hauntings. Although many people refer to it as the Judge Amidon Monument, it is actually the Pioneer Memorial. A stone marker at the base explains its purpose:

> The Pioneer Memorial honors the early settlers who faced the harsh and lonely prairie, the ferocity of the elements, and the uncertainty of their fate in this new land. Between 1856 when Sioux Falls City was platted and 1889 when South Dakota achieved statehood, they built homes, farms, and businesses and planted their family roots in Minnehaha County.

Saint Michael Cemetery is nearby, and some speculate that the mysterious lights and other haunting activities are actually connected to the burials there.

Washington Pavilion

Location: Sioux Falls, Minnehaha County, South Dakota
Official Name: Washington Pavilion of Arts and Science
Address: 301 South Main Avenue, Sioux Falls, SD 57104-6311
Toll Free: 1-877-WashPav
Ticket Hotline: (605) 367-6000
Administration and other areas: (605) 367-7397
Email: info@washingtonpavilion.org
Website: www.washpav.org

Ghost Lore

This stately edifice has been the center of learning in Sioux Falls for nearly a century. First as a school, then as a pavilion. Some even believe we can learn a thing or two about the afterlife in these halls.

The story is told about a construction worker who accidentally fell to his death in an open elevator shaft when the building was being renovated. People will sometimes encounter the spectral revenant while riding the elevators. They see him standing in the elevator when they board it, but after they reach their desired floor, they realize that while they had their backs to him, he vanished into thin air.

Haunting activity also occurs in the theater. Stagehands report that the ghost will tamper with the soundboard, lights, and props. Whether this is the same spirit that haunts the elevators is unknown.

People also report other strange phenomena:

- Sound of phantom footsteps in the corridor.

- Sense of being watched and followed.

- Feelings of apprehension.

History

1895 – Sioux Falls Central High School began with an enrollment of 20 students. The name was later changed to McKinley High School.

1904 – The student enrollment quickly outgrew the building and construction began on a new school.

1908 – February 14. Construction was completed, and the new building was christened with a bottle of Minnehaha Springs water as "Washington High School," with 328 students attending the first day of classes on George Washington's birthday.

1922 – The South Wing was added due to the increase in student enrollment.

1932 – The North Wing was added.

1935 – The center unit was completed.

1965 – Due to overcrowding, a second school, Lincoln High School, opened.

1992 – Further overcrowding required the construction of a larger building. The new Washington High School opened at 501 North Sycamore Avenue with an enrollment of 1,439 students. The 256,000 square-foot building cost $15 million and sits on 40 acres.

1999 – June. After months of renovation, the old high school building reopened as the Washington Pavilion, a state-of-the-art educational and entertainment facility. It featured the Visual Arts Center, Kirby Science Discovery Center, Wells Fargo CineDome Theater and Husby Performing Arts Center.

Investigation

There are two elevators in the pavilion. It is not known which one is supposed to be haunted. Perhaps the ghost rides both elevators.

The Washington Pavilion employees are reluctant to discuss the haunting activies and are concerned about children being fearful.

Although we found numerous people who could verify the haunting activity, we were unable to confirm the story of the alleged death of a worker. Our investigation is ongoing in this case.

Spirit Mound

Location: Vermillion, Clay County, South Dakota
Mailing Address: Spirit Mound Historic Prairie, 28771 482nd
Avenue, Canton, SD 57013-6205
Phone: (605) 987-2263
Email: NewtonHills@state.sd.us

Directions: From Highway 19 turn north for five miles.

Ghost Lore

Spirit Mound sits majestically upon 320 acres of pristine prairie land. Take the ¾ mile walk to the summit and you will be standing in the same spot where the famous adventurers Lewis and Clark stood over 200 years ago. Surrounded by native plants and prairie grass it is easy to believe that you are the only living person in the whole world. However, as you look around Spirit Mound you may find that you are certainly not alone.

History

Late 1700s – French fur traders move throughout the area.

1804 – The Lewis and Clark expedition made a nine-mile trek from their camp along the Vermillion River to visit the place local Native Americans called *Paha Wakan* or Spirit Mountain.

1974 – Spirit Mound was placed on the National Registry of Historic Places.

1976 – The Nature Conservancy acquired the preserve. They used controlled fires, cleared the drainage, and removed non-native plants from the area.

2001 – Spirit Mound was privately owned. However, several groups including the National Park Service, the South Dakota Department of Fish, Game, and Parks, and the Spirit Mound Trust acquired the land. The groups set a goal of restoring the area to its native settings. The plan included seeding the area with native

prairie species.

Currently – The preserve is open to research and researchers and is being closely managed to provide a home for native mammals, invertebrates, and vegetation.

Investigation

Spirit Mound was known to the local Native Americans as *Paha Wakan.*

The Native Americans of the area believed that the Spirit Mound was inhabited by little 'Deavels' that were armed with arrows. These devils would attack any outsider that was brave enough to venture to the mound.

Clark wrote in his journal that these devils were said to be 18 inches tall and in human form with remarkably large heads. Clark went on to write that the devils were also said to be extremely watchful and armed with razor sharp arrows in which they were experts at using. Clark was told that the devils would kill all persons who were so hardy as to attempt to approach the hill. Clark was also told that many Indians had suffered by these little people.

Today many people report hearing sounds of 'people' running through the area, yet no one can be found.

The Dare: If you climb to the top of the mound, you will encounter the little people.

NORTHERN SOUTH DAKOTA

Easton Castle

Location: Aberdeen, Brown County, South Dakota
Address: 1210 Second Avenue Northwest, Aberdeen, SD
57401-2649

Not open to the public. Please, do not trespass.

Ghost Lore

Does the ghost of Dorothy Gale from *The Wizard of Oz* haunt a castle in South Dakota? This might sound like a nonsensical question, considering Dorothy was a fictional character who hailed from Kansas. So, some elucidation is in order here. It is said that L. Frank Baum, author of *The Wonderful Wizard of Oz,* based his character of Dorothy on his young niece who lived in Aberdeen. This real-life Dorothy worked for the wealthy Easton family in Aberdeen and was a frequent guest at their yellow-brick house known as the Easton Castle. The Eastons always showed hospitality towards "Dorothy," making her feel at home in their castle. Over the years, she spent so much time there, it eventually became her home away from home.

For many years, local residents have been terrified of this ominous-looking castle and believed it to be haunted. It was so scary, even trick-or-treaters were afraid to go up to the door on Halloween.

According to rumors, the ghost of "Dorothy" still hangs out in the castle. They say she haunts the upper-floor of the house and has been known to walk the grounds. It seems that even after death, "there's no place like home."

The Castle has been appropriately described as a house of history, mystery, and legend.

• It is rumored Mrs. Easton died in the house and haunts it.

Tower room where a ghost was seen.

- Somebody once saw the ghost of a woman on the third floor.

- Another person was chased inside the house by a knife-wielding spirit.

- Owners have reported hearing creaking floorboards and footsteps in the hallway.

History of Easton Castle

1886 or 1889 – The "Bliss House," a 30-room, three-story, Queen Anne style house, was built on a 13-acre lot on West Hill. The owner, C.A. Bliss, was President of the Territorial Board of Agriculture and owner of the Artesian Hotel. He was probably the wealthiest man in Aberdeen.

C.F. Easton and Eva Easton

Photos on these two pages were provided courtesy of Sam, Jacintha, and Tandy Holman.

1892 or 1893 – The house was purchased by Carroll Francis Easton, a New York businessman. C.F. Easton was the secretary of three Building & Loan Associations. He was remembered as the man who encouraged people to plant trees in Aberdeen. An oil

painting by his wife, Eva B. Easton, still hangs on the wall of the courting room. One of his business partners was L. Frank Baum's brother-in-law, T.C. Gage. Gage's daughter, Matilda Jewell Gage, worked for them as a business secretary and underwriter.

Bliss House

1902 or 1904 – Originally a wood structure, at the urging of Easton's son Russell the house was given a Jacobian-style brick veneer. Easton converted it from a Queen Anne to an English Manor style house, and covered it with yellow bricks. From this time forward, it was known as the "Easton Castle." The house became a showplace of Aberdeen. Baum's nieces, Matilda and Leslie, frequently attended the tea parties, dances, and dinners thrown at the Castle.

1935 – May 10. C.F. Easton died at the age of 78.

1944 – Eva Easton died.

1945-1965 – Their son Russell Easton locked himself up in the

The House as Matilda and Leslie knew it.

house, becoming an eccentric recluse. People only saw a single light burning in a third-story window. "No trespassing" signs went up, and those who infringed on his privacy were shot at. During these two decades the castle fell into disrepair and gained a reputation for being haunted.

1965 – Russell Easton died at the age of 60.

1967 – Veterinarian Sam J. Holman (known as "Doc") & his wife Jacintha Holman (known as "Jack") purchased the castle to use as both a veterinarian clinic and private residence. They currently live there with their daughter Tandy. Every Halloween, for almost 20 years, the Holman family used to decorate the castle as a haunted mansion and grant "castle tours" to the public.

1972 – The house was listed on the National Register of Historical Places.

History of L. Frank Baum

1856 – May 15. Lyman Frank Baum was born to Benjamin and Cynthia Ann Stanton Baum in Chittenango, New York.

1882 – February 8. Baum's niece, Leslie Gage, was born in Syracuse, New York to Charles Henry (1816-1892) and Helen Leslie Gage (1845-1933).

1882 – November 9. Baum married Maud Gage, daughter of the famous women's suffrage activist, Matilda Joslyn Gage.

1886 – April 22. Baum's niece, Matilda Jewell Gage, was born.

1888 – July. Baum and his wife moved to Aberdeen. For a short time he owned a store, "Baum's Bazaar," that went bankrupt and later he was the owner and editor of *The Aberdeen Saturday Pioneer*, which also went bankrupt in 1891.

1890 – April. Baum gave the first public tour of the Bliss House.

In *The Aberdeen Saturday Pioneer,* he wrote: ". . . a large and merry company boarded the White Wings bus Thursday evening and drove to the spacious mansion of C.A. Bliss on West Hill. As the guests roamed through the elegantly appointed and well-furnished rooms, they could not forebear uttering exclamations of surprise at the novel sights that met their gaze on every hand."

1891 – May. Baum moved his family to Chicago.

1896 – Baum wrote his first children's book, *Mother Goose in Prose* (published in 1897). The heroine of the story was named Dorothy.

1898 – June 11. Baum's niece, Dorothy Louise Gage, was born to Sophie Jewel and Thomas Clarkson Gage in Bloomington, Illinois. She died five months later on November 11, 1898 and was buried in Evergreen Memorial Cemetery.

1900 – Baum published *The Wonderful Wizard of Oz,* the first in a series of thirteen novels. His description of Kansas in the book is said to be based on his experiences in drought-stricken South Dakota.

1919 – May 6. Baum died, aged 62, and was buried in the Forest Lawn Memorial Park Cemetery in Glendale, California.

1966 – July 8. Baum's niece, Leslie Gage, aged 84, died in Winona, Minnesota.

1986 – February. Baum's niece, Matilda Jewell Gage, died at the age of 99.

Investigation

Touring this grand old house was like stepping into the past. Most of the woodwork, wallpaper, flooring, and fixtures were original, along with much of the furnishings. Even some of the books, magazines, and artwork were more than a century old. If any house was going to be haunted, you would certainly expect this one to be. The owners even had us sign a guestbook that dated back to the 1880s and contained thousands of signatures.

One of the first things we noticed about the interior of the house was that the decorative carvings on the woodwork in the dining

room and sitting room were unfinished. This is just one of the many mysteries of the house. Several theories have been offered. Perhaps sample pieces were used, or the woodworker was fired for drinking on the job, or the Eastons couldn't afford to complete the work, or Mr. Easton did the work himself, but never found the time to finish it.

The Holmans, a family of fervent Democrats, talked about how they made headlines in 1982. Then Republican Governor Bill Janklow threatened them with a defamation lawsuit over a poster they displayed in their upstairs hall. Apparently Janklow did not believe the Holman's home was their castle—so to speak. He maintained that because the Easton Castle is listed with the National Register of Historical Places, it is a public place. The Holmans removed the offending anti-Janklow poster, immediately replacing it with a copy of the Bill of Rights—with the Fourth Amendment highlighted! Later, both the National Trust and the National Register ruled against Janklow, determining the Easton Castle to not be a public place.

The family talked about the time L. Frank Baum's niece, Matilda Jewell Gage, visited them in the 1970s. Gage reminisced about the times she and her cousin Leslie played and visited in the Easton Caslte. They used to fantasize that it was their home. She also talked about Dorothy Gale.

Over the years, several women have claimed to be the inspiration for the character of Dorothy Gale; however, the Baum family has always maintained that Dorothy was named after no one in particular. Apparently L. Frank Baum selected the name simply because he liked it.

Some claim Dorothy was named for Baum's niece, Dorothy Louise Gage, who died in infancy in 1898, but Baum had already named a character Dorothy in his first children's book, *Mother Goose in Prose*, written two years prior.

It is possible the character—not the name—was based on somebody Baum knew. His niece Matilda Jewell Gage always claimed

ne inspiration for Dorothy, but most people say it was the
e Leslie Gage. In the books, Dorothy's age is never given, but, based on the illustrations in the books, she could be as young as six or as old as twelve. Most people think she was supposed to be between eight and ten. When *The Wonderful Wizard of Oz* was published, Leslie was eight years old, but Matilda was only four. If the character was modeled after one of them, it most likely was Leslie.

Does the ghost of Leslie Gage haunt the Easton Castle? The Holmans doubt it, but they did tell us about an incident that happened there in 1981. Maintenance man Bruce Lindvall was doing work at the Easton Castle when he had a terrifying experience convincing him that although he wasn't in Kansas anymore, Dorothy might be in South Dakota.

Lindvall and another worker had gone up to the unoccupied third floor of the house and entered the circular room in the tower. Upon opening the door, they saw the rope chandelier rapidly spinning like a pendulum in a circular movement. Nobody else was in the room or in the house at the time. There were no open windows or sources of a draft. Both men quickly vacated the house. They jumped into their truck, and in his rearview mirror Lindvall distinctly saw a young woman dressed in a 1910s style, long dress and wearing a wide-brimmed, floppy hat. He gunned the engine and sped off. Neither man returned to the castle.

Matilda Gage was still alive at that time, not dying until five years later; but Leslie Gage, who most likely was the inspiration for Dorothy Gale, had been dead for 15 years. Could the two men have encountered an apparition of Leslie Gage? Nobody knows for certain.

The owners of the house insist it is not haunted, but other people would disagree and quote the Cowardly Lion: "I do believe in spooks. I do believe in spooks. I do! I do! I do!"

Lamont House

Location: Aberdeen, Brown County, South Dakota
Address: 519 South Arch Street, Aberdeen, SD 57401-4444

Directions: Corner of Sixth Avenue Southeast and South Arch Street. It is the meeting place for Alcoholics Anonymous groups.

Ghost Lore

The large, yellow Queen Anne home on Arch Street is a popular landmark in Aberdeen, known to locals as the "Lamont House." Of all the Victorian house styles, Queen Anne is considered to be the most elaborate and the most eccentric.

In the 1880s and 1890s, Queen Anne architecture became popular at the beginning of the Industrial Revolution. With the new technology, factories were able to manufacture precut architectural pieces and quickly ship them across the country by train. Builders were able to combine these prefab parts to create innovative homes, enabling many wealthy businessmen and industrialists to build lavish homes that looked like castles.

The story around town is that a 27-year-old industrialist who grew up in this house met an untimely death due to a hunting accident. Today his spirit walks the halls of his boyhood home, tormented by the injustice of having his life cut short just as he was starting a family and business.

History

1862 – Byron Cook "B.C." Lamont was born.

1866 – Anna Maria Brereton was born.

1885 – The house at 519 South Arch Street was built for C.F. Easton (see page 72).

1887 – B.C. and Anna were married. B.C. was a pioneer lawyer and owned real estate and mortgage banking businesses.

1888 – Maurice Brereton Lamont, their only child, was born to B.C. and Anna.

1893 – B.C. and Anna purchased the house at 519 South Arch Street.

1910 – Maurice graduated from the University of Wisconsin and in a joint venture with his friend, W.O. Wells, founded the Wells-Lamont Glove Company in Aberdeen manufacturing work gloves.

1912 – B.C. and Anna built the house at 515 South Arch Street as a wedding gift for Maurice and his new wife Margaret.

1915 – November 26. Maurice was killed in a tragic hunting accident at Sand Lake. His widow raised their two kids, William and Robert, alone. She died in 1973.

1964 – The house was purchased by the Alano Society.

Investigation

The big, yellow house is hard not to notice, but most people have probably driven by it without realizing that on top of the northwest turret is a large glass goblet turned upside down. It symbolizes the end of drinking for the AA members who meet there.

- Several people report feeling uneasy when they enter the house.

The turret with the goblet

- People have heard ghostly footsteps and other strange sounds on the staircase and on the second floor.

- One person related the terrifying experience of hearing a disembodied voice tell them to "get out!"

- Most commonly reported is the sound of a baby crying, coming from one of the second-story rooms. Although possible, it is not known for certain if the Lamonts had a child who died in infancy.

Ward Hotel

Location: Aberdeen, Brown County, South Dakota
Official Name: Alonzo Ward Plaza Suites
Address: 104 South Main Street, Aberdeen, SD 57401-4137
Phone: (605) 225-6100 or (605) 725-5550

Ghost Lore

It is not uncommon to find hotels that are haunted, generally because they are often the tallest building in town, and despondent people can easily check into a room on the upper floor and end their life by leaping from an open window.

As rumor has it, in the 1930s, a traveler checked in at the Alonzo Ward Hotel and checked out by nose-diving from a fifth-floor window. Since that tragic day, the room has been haunted by a dispirited spirit eternally trapped by their grief and sorrow in netherworld accommodations with no room service.

History

1861 – Alonzo LaRue Ward Sr. was born in Lima, Ohio.

1883 – A.L. Ward saved up $100 and moved to Huron where he worked in a restaurant.

1884 – November 5. A.L. Ward and his wife Caroline (nee Paulhamus) had a son, Alonzo "Bud" LaRue Ward Jr.

1885 – A.L. Ward moved from Huron to Aberdeen with only five cents in his pocket and opened a lunch stand on the spot currently occupied by the hotel coffee shop. From this humble beginning, the 24-year-old man began his business. It quickly grew into a good sized restaurant and featured Aberdeen's first commercial ice cream freezer.

1897 – A.L. Ward built the three-story, 100-room, red brick Ward Hotel.

1926 – Thanksgiving Day. The hotel is completely destroyed by fire. It took firefighters from Aberdeen, Redfield, and Groton over ten hours and nearly one million gallons of water to quench the blaze, but not before it did $300,000 worth of damage.

1928 – A.L. Ward built a six story, 130-room, fireproof hotel on the same site as the original. It featured a mezzanine with a two-story ballroom and stage. This one was named the "Alonzo Ward Hotel." It opened on May 15th. Mayor John Wade was the first guest to sign in.

1929 – January. A.L. Ward died.

1948 – A.L. Ward's wife, Caroline died. Their son "Bud" continued to manage the hotel.

1935 – January 21. Aberdeen's first radio station, KABR, began broadcasting from the sixth floor of the hotel.

1964 – June 1. The Ward family sold the hotel to Mr. and Mrs. Louis Long Jr.

1969 – The hotel was sold to the Ward Hotel Corporation, a division of F. W. Haterscheidt and Co.

1981 – The hotel was purchased by Dr. Harvey Hart and his wife Velna and Attorney Tom Tonner and his wife Susan.

1982 – Alonzo Ward Hotel was added to the National Register of Historic Places.

1984 – February. Alonzo "Bud" Ward Jr. died.

2004 – Blackstone development group spent $6 million on a restoration project for the hotel. They renovated the second-floor ballroom and mezzanine, added eight rooms on the second floor, built 15 condominiums on the upper floors, and a fitness spa on the lower level.

Among the many guests who stayed at the hotel were President William Howard Taft, entertainer Jack Benny, and then-Senator John F. Kennedy.

Investigation

We spoke with a bartender who had worked for the hotel for over 15 years. He was able to verify that there was a suicide at the hotel. Many people are convinced the hotel is haunted, and over the years, both customers and staff have reported ghostly activity in the room on the fifth-floor.

The employee recounted an incident that happened one night while he was bartending. A young teacher, who knew nothing about the suicide or haunting, was traveling to a convention and spent the night at the Alonzo Ward Hotel. Exhausted from a long day of driving, she was relaxing on the bed when she heard a noise in the bathroom. Her horrified eyes were big as saucers as she watched the doorknob slowly begin to turn, and the door opened, presumably on its own accord. The terrified teacher, fearing there was an intruder in her room, looked inside and found the bathroom to be empty.

The woman, ashen-faced and trembling, told her story to the bartender as she downed a couple of stiff drinks to calm her nerves. Upon questioning her further, he realized she had checked into the

haunted room. Straightaway the school teacher packed her bags and dashed from the hotel without spending the night. She found lodging elsewhere, but over the years many brave individuals have stayed in the hotel, eagerly hoping to spend the night in a haunted room.

Shupick Park

Location: Eagle Butte, Dewey County, South Dakota

Directions: In Eagle Butte, turn south off Highway 212 onto Willow Street. The park will be on the right.

Ghost Lore

Encountering a specter can be a chilling experience, but nothing is more chilling than coming face-to-face with a frozen corpse strolling through a park late at night.

It is said that one winter, several years ago, a homeless woman sought shelter at the local baseball park and died alone and cold in the middle of the night. The next day, local residents were shocked to find her frozen body behind the fence.

Since that tragic day, people have reported that if you walk through the park late at night you can sometimes hear her frail voice calling out to you. Others report hearing her screaming, sobbing, or moaning.

A few people have had the terrifying experience of seeing a lone figure meandering aimlessly through the park late after dark. Upon closer inspection, they discover a walking cadaver, complete with icy white skin and dark sunken eyes.

History

The park, named after local resident Louis Shupick, has been in Eagle Butte since the 1940s.

Investigation

We spoke with a grandson of Louis Shupick who confirmed that the story of the woman's death is true and happened about 10-15 years ago. According to his recollection, there was no sign of foul play. She was apparently intoxicated and froze to death in the ball field behind the fence.

Coal Mines

Location: Firesteel, Dewey County, South Dakota

Directions: From Firesteel, take 20 north, turn left on 3d. Quarry is a half mile down road on left.

Ghost Lore

It seems logical that a ghost town should have ghosts. Such is the case with Firesteel. When coal was discovered in this part of South Dakota, this little town quickly grew and became prosperous. However, tragedy struck in the 1930s when a coal mine explosion killed over 100 miners. Since that day, the mine shafts have been haunted and the ghosts of the dead miners have driven away most of the townspeople.

If you stand near the mine shafts, you can hear the ghostly voices of the miners and the sounds of their picks and shovels.

History

1875 – The town was started by Israel Green and others.

1907 – Andrew Traversie and William Benoist were the first people to officially mine the Firesteel coal fields.

1911 – The first real commercial mining began with a company owned by Fred Hammersly and Charles Lindt.

1923 – The Firesteel Coal Company was formed. They hired over 60 workers and produced 40,000 to 50,000 tons of coal per year.

1933 – The South Dakota Relief Agency started a strip-mine operation.

1934 – The South Dakota Relief Agency strip-mine shut down.

1969 – The Firesteel Coal Company went out of business.

1981 – Reclamation began to bring the land back to a beneficial use.

Investigation

A quick lesson on coal mining is necessary. There are two principle systems of coal mining: **strip** (surface) mining and **deep** (underground).

Strip mining, a form of quarrying, is only done when the stratum of coal is near the surface of the ground. Power shovels and draglines are used to remove the overburden (rock and soil) that covers the seam. Then smaller shovels are used to load the coal into trucks.

Deep mining is done when the seam is much deeper beneath the surface, and involves digging a vertical or inclined shaft into the ground to reach the coal. The coal is blasted with explosives and carried out by a conveyor belt.

What we found at Firesteel was an open mine. There are no mine shafts here, and there were never any mine explosions. Although individual workers may have been killed here in the past, there is no evidence that an accident resulted in the loss of over 100 men.

Also, our historical investigation determined that, as is common with mining communities, the population moved on when the mines closed down, and there were no other jobs to be found.

Standing atop the hills and looking into the open quarry can inspire an inexplicable fear or uneasiness. The panoramic openness and extreme stillness seem to heighten the senses, and a lot of people do report hearing strange sounds and voices coming from the pits where so many used to labor. Those brave enough to remain in the quarry after dark, claim the voices become even more readily discernible.

Isabel

Location: Isabel, Dewey County, South Dakota

Ghost Lore

Burress Feeds. The Burress Feeds store is located at 224 Main Street, but the original store is located west of there. According to rumors, a young preteen Indian girl haunts the old store. She was an unfortunate victim of smallpox in the early 1900s. If you walk past the abandoned store late at night, you can hear her inside the building crying and calling out for her mother.

Post Office. People report seeing strange things in the window of the post office at 200 Main Street. Sometimes, while standing outside and looking into the post office through the window, people will see somebody inside, but, upon entering the lobby, they are shocked to discover it is empty.

Other times they might be standing inside the post office looking out the window and see the reflection of somebody standing directly behind them giving them an evil stare. When they turn around, nobody is there.

A story is told that a woman went to the post office one evening to get her mail. There were no employees there, but the lobby was open so people could check their mail boxes. The woman got her mail, but when she went to leave, she discovered the door was locked, and she could not get out. Nobody heard her cries for help, and she was trapped in the building overnight. When she was discovered the next morning, the door easily opened and was not found to be locked, but the woman was so traumatized she had to be hospitalized. For several days, she was catatonic and blathering about ghosts.

Isabel Post Office

Rodeo Grounds. The rodeo grounds are located on the west end of town, and people who have visited the grounds late at night report hearing strange sounds and voices. In an abandoned, dilapidated house nearby, they will sometimes see a mysterious light in one of the windows, despite the fact that the house has no electricity. If you walk past the old white house after dark, the light will sometimes exit through the window and move towards you. At this point, most people begin running, but they say the spook light will follow them all the way to Main Street.

School. The elementary, junior high, and high school are housed in the same building at 410 North Main Street. Students talk about a young Indian boy who was accidentally locked in the janitorial closet and suffocated. Children sometimes say they can hear him in the janitor room. Often the school custodian will open the door to get cleaning supplies and be startled to find the small ghost standing in there. The child quickly vanishes into thin air.

Isabel School

Rodeo Grounds

Haunted House near Rodeo Grounds

History

The Milwaukee Railroad created this town in 1910. It was one of three communities that were spaced every 20 miles along railroad tracks that originated in Mobridge. The president of the railroad named the town for one of his two daughters. Because of the Homesead Act, settlers quickly moved into the area. The post office was started July 18, 1910, and the town was incorporated April 4, 1911. The rodeo has been in town since 1961. The railroad closed down in 1979.

Investigation

The town has a population of under 240 people. About 120 students are enrolled in the school. One-third of the population is Native American. When we first visited the town, what struck us as strange was the fact that all the streets were deserted. It was a beautiful, sunny day, yet nobody was out jogging, or walking their

Burress Feeds

dog, or riding a bicycle. It truly seemed like a ghost town. It was not until several hours later that we actually saw any people.

- The school denies that any children died in the janitor room.

- Mr. Burress sold his store years ago and moved to Nebraska. Although the original store is boarded up, people still claim to hear the sounds of the little girl inside.

- Postal workers deny that the post office is haunted, but many residents would disagree.

- Several people claim to have encountered the mysterious light at the rodeo grounds.

Fort Sisseton

Location: Lake City, Marshall County, South Dakota
Official Name: Fort Sisseton State Historic Park
Address: 11545 434th Avenue, Lake City, SD 57247-6119
Phone: (605) 448-5474 or (605) 448-5701
Fax: (605) 448-5572
Email: RoyLake@state.sd.us
Camping Reservations: 1-800-710-CAMP
Camping: www.CampSD.com

Directions: Located 10 miles southwest of Lake City off US Hwy 10.

Ghost Lore

Does a lone sentry still stand guard at Fort Sisseton? Several of the employees and visitors to the historic fort seem to think so.

- A visitor was touring the officers' quarters when she felt invisible hands grip her neck and attempt to strangle her.

- Phantom footsteps have been heard in some of the buildings.

- Visitors have a sense of being watched and followed.

- Mysterious lights have been seen.

- Apparitions have appeared.

History

1864 – Fort Wadsworth was established in the Dakota Territory by Wisconsin and Minnesota Volunteers during the Civil War. It served to protect wagon trains from Sioux Indian attacks as emigrants traveled west to the goldfields in Idaho and Montana. The fort was called the "Peacekeeper of the Dakota Kettle Lake region."

1876 – It was renamed Fort Sisseton after the friendly Sisseton Indian tribe who helped protect it from attack by unfriendly tribes.

1889 – June 1st. The fort was officially closed. Control was transferred from the Army to the State.

1935-39 – The fort was restored by the Works Project Administration (WPA).

1959 – It reopened as a historic park. The South Dakota Department of Game, Fish, and Parks restored it and continues its preservation.

1973 – It was added to the National Register of Historic Places.

Investigation

The fort is built on an ancient Indian burial mound. When military personnel put up the first flagpole in 1864, they inadvertently disturbed an Indian grave.

A quarter mile from the fort is the Fort Sisseton Cemetery. Forty-four people were buried there. The bodies of these soldiers and their families were later exhumed and reburied in Little Big Horn National Cemetery. A single wooden cross marks the original cemetery.

A set designer, involved in one of the fort's plays, was working there alone late at night. Through the window of the officers' quarters she spied a woman dressed in white, holding a candle, and walking from window to window. A local historian brought to notice the fact that there might be a historical basis for the strange behavior of this ghost. During the fort's 1879 bedbug infestation, it was common for women and maids to be up every night burning the bugs from the walls with the flame of a candle.

What are most commonly reported at Fort Sisseton are mysterious lights. It is not uncommon for local residents to be driving past the fort late at night during the season when the park is closed and to see bright lights near the buildings or shining from the windows. The lights can be either moving or fixed. Sometimes they change

Sica Hollow

Location: Lake City, Marshall County, South Dakota
Official Name: Sica Hollow State Park
Address: 11545 Northside Drive, Lake City, SD 57247-6142
Phone: 605-448-5701
Email: RoyLake@state.sd.us

Directions: Located 15 miles northwest of Sisseton, off S.D. Highway 10, within 35 miles of I-29.

Ghost Lore

In 1820, Washington Irving published the popular ghost story, "The Legend of Sleepy Hollow." As it turns out, South Dakota has its own spooky hollow full of legends. A place known as Sica Hollow. This wooded area, with rugged hills and deep ravines, seems out of place in the middle of the prairie. Although traditional Native American spirituality considered the earth to be sacred, legend has it that the local Indians believed this place to be evil and avoided it like the plague. They thought the bogs contained the flesh and blood of their ancestors, and they feared the evil spirits that lived in the woods.

According to a popular Indian legend, at one time a tribe did live peacefully in the hollow, until they were visited by an evil white man named "Hand" who turned their young men into cold-blooded killers. A shaman petitioned *Wanka Tanka* (the "Great Spirit") for help, and a thunderbird came to their rescue. The thunderbird created a flood and used its wings to push Hand into the water. Creeping vines reached up from beneath the water and restrained Hand by his ankles. The floodwaters continued to rise until they reached his mouth. The thunderbird's *coup de grace* was to use its mighty talons to rip out the eyeballs of Hand, preventing him from ever seeing the happy hunting ground. Unfortunately, the flood sent to deliver the people inadvertently killed all, save one young girl. It is believed the ghost of Hand haunts the hollow, and he hides in the forest with gouged out eye sockets.

When white settlers first moved into the region, they too feared the hollow and prudently looked elsewhere to live.

There are two cemeteries in the park: Roy Cemetery and Saint Benedict Cemetery. Both are rumored to be haunted.

In recent years there have been reports of a Bigfoot creature inhabiting the forest. Stories are told that in the 1970s a group of hikers disappeared in Sica Hollow. Search parties were organized, but, after several days of searching, the missing people were never found. Could they have been the victims of the Bigfoot?

The Dare: If you spend the night in the woods, you will hear ghostly voices and chanting. If fortune is with you, you might encounter an Indian spirit; however, if misfortune is with you, you might encounter a Bigfoot or, even worse, the ghost of Hand.

History

20,000 years ago the last glacier receded and left strange rolling hills in the middle of the plains.

900-1300 CE – The Woodland Culture lived in the region.

1840s – The first white settlers, the Roy (French Roi) family arrived in the area.

1971 – The Trail of the Spirits, a self-guided interpretive foot trail, was designated as a National Recreation Trail.

Investigation

When the Sioux first visited the hollow, they named it "Sica" (pronounced she-chee) meaning evil or bad. It is not true that they avoided this area. During the harsh winters on the prairie, they would apparently seek the shelter of these forested ravines. Currently Indians still visit Sica Hollow to perform sacred ceremonies.

Park officials dismiss the stories of missing hikers and Bigfoot sightings as being untrue. Although they acknowledge the fact that strange things have been seen and heard in the park, they attempt to find rational, naturalistic explanations for them.

- The gurgling, red bogs, which Indians believed to contain the flesh and blood of their ancestors, are explained to be peat and moss that get their red color from iron deposits in the water.

- The moans, groans, and screams heard in the forest are rationalized as the sounds of trapped gases escaping from the muddy bogs.

- Spook lights seen in the bogs are known as will-o'-the-wisps, and are assumed to be a flame caused by the spontaneous combustion of methane emitted by rotting organic matter in the mud. Lights seen in the woods are called foxfire. They are supposedly produced by bioluminescent fungi found on rotting wood.

Although the explanation for the coloration of the bogs proves adequate, the other rationalizations fall short.

Sounds. People who hear the sounds in the woods describe them as distinctly human vocalizations. In addition, some of the noises are unmistakably the rhythmic percussion of drumming. Although the possibility exists that local Indians could be in the hollow performing a ceremony, no Indians are ever found to be present.

Foxfire. The December 1, 1924 issue of the Lincoln, Nebraska *Night Journal* reported a rash of spook light sightings across South Dakota, particularly in the vicinity of Madison in Lake County and the eastern parts of Pennington County.

One businessman reported he saw a light coming down the road toward his car at a breakneck speed. Thinking it was an oncoming vehicle, he quickly veered into the ditch to avoid an accident, but the light mysteriously vanished at the point of collision.

The article noted that the lights had been seen in the past, but they were more frequent and of greater brilliance that year than ever before. In certain hot spots the mysterious lights could be seen regularly, and often people from surrounding communities would drive out there nightly to witness the phenomenon. Many people were terrified and believed it was a sign of the end of the world.

The mobility of the spook lights completely refutes the idea of them being bioluminescent fungi on a stationary, rotting tree stump.

It is a little farfetched to suggest a glowing fungus could run a car off the road by barreling down the highway.

Will-o'-the-wisp. Will-o'-the-wisp was originally "Will with the wisp." A wisp being a small bundle of straw twisted together and used as a torch. Another popular name was jack-o'-lantern, originally meaning "Jack with a lantern." The names derived from the belief that a mischievous spirit was attempting to lead astray unwary travelers at night.

In 1730, Isaac Newton was the first to propose the marsh gas (methane) explanation. Although this trite theory has been passed down from generation to generation, without being questioned or adequately tested, a number of serious objections can be raised against it.

- In the lab it has been shown that pure methane does not spontaneously inflame. It has been suggested phosphine (PH_3), another gas produced in the bogs, could ignite the methane, but pure phosphine is also not self-igniting. In 1980, tests conducted by Dr. Alan Mills, a geologist at Leicester University, failed to replicate a will-o'-the-wisp under laboratory conditions using methane and phosphine. In order for it to ignite spontaneously, it had to be mixed with a small amount of phosphorous tetrahydride (P_2H_4) which resulted in a bright, green flame, a large amount of smoke, and a distinct odor. Will-o'-the-wisps do not produce stinking, green clouds of smoke.

- Bubbles of methane can be ignited with a lighted match, but the burning gas usually emits a popping sound. No sounds are associated with the will-o'-the-wisps.

- When phosphine (aka hydrogen phosphide) burns, it produces distinct vortical rings of smoke that are never seen in association with a will-o'-the-wisp.

- The combustion of methane would produce a yellow flame and generate heat. Will-o'-the-wisps are bluish (sometimes reddish or whitish) in appearance, and reportedly cold to the touch.

- Witnesses describe the lights as having a motive or sentient quality. The lights' behavior suggests some kind of low-order intelligence. Sometimes the lights appear to follow people, to move away from them, or to interact with them.

- Trenches have been dug through peat bogs, releasing huge quantities of swamp gas, yet there were no ignitions, and no will-o'-the-wisps appeared.

- They frequently disappear, only to reappear nearby.

- A bubble of methane would burn for only a few seconds, but the will-o'-the-wisps can maintain their size and shape sometimes for several hours.

- Will-o'-the-wisps are not always found near bogs. They have also been sighted in mountains, sandstone uplands, fields, and above rivers. Many times they are seen in cemeteries and referred to as "corpse candles."

- Ignited methane exiting from a marsh would be a fixed flame. It is not uncommon for will-o'-the-wisps to move. They have even been known to follow the same path night after night. They are not disturbed by a breeze and can even move against the wind. Occasionally witnesses report seeing two or more lights moving in perfect symmetry with each other.

Mc Laughlin

Location: Mc Laughlin, Corson County, South Dakota
Directions: Located 29 miles from Mobridge.

Ghost Lore

Often we use the interjection, "bingo!" to express something surprising or unexpected, and it is a fitting expression to describe the things that happen at the Bear Soldier Jackpot Bingo hall and other places in Mc Laughlin.

Bingo Hall. Bear Soldier Jackpot Bingo, located at 1 Sale Barn Road, is alleged to be haunted because it was built on a cemetery.

Devil's Butte. On the butte directly south of town, people have seen the Devil himself standing at the pinnacle.

Haunted Road. Several years ago a man was killed in a gruesome car accident just outside of town. The motorist was decapitated, and his head was found in a nearby pond. Several people have seen a headless apparition walking the road at night in search of his head.

High School. The high school, located at 601 South Main Street, is said to be haunted. Several years ago a janitor was mopping the floor near the swimming pool when he slipped and struck his head. He died instantly. Since his death, students will sometimes hear his familiar whistling in the hallway. Some teenagers have even seen apparitions of him busily at work, mopping the school floors.

A second ghost haunts the school gymnasium. A popular basketball coach died unexpectedly, and since his death strange things have happened in the school gym. When the lights are shut off in the gym, students have heard the sound of a basketball being bounced across the floor. When the lights are turned on, the room

Bear Soldier Jackpot Bingo

is found to be empty. Others have reported having basketballs thrown at them, yet nobody was there.

Historic McLaughlin House. The house is said to be haunted by Major James McLaughlin.

History of Mc Laughlin

Mc Laughlin was named for Major James McLaughlin. This small town, located on the Standing Rock Reservation, has a population of about 775 people, nearly half of whom are Native American.

1908 – July 13. The post office was established.

1909 – The town was incorporated and named after Major James McLaughlin.

Devil's Butte

History of James McLaughlin

1842 – James McLaughlin was born in Ontario, Canada.

1871 – January 28. He married Marie L. Graham at Mendota, Minnesota. Her maternal grandmother, *Ha-za-ho-ta-win,* was a full-blooded Sioux of the Medawakanton Band.

1871 – July 1. McLaughlin was employed as a blacksmith and general overseer of the new Fort Totten and trained to be an Indian agent.

1876 – McLaughlin was appointed as an Indian agent at the Devil's Lake Agency.

1881 – McLaughlin was transferred to Standing Rock Reservation. As the superintendent of the reservation, he assisted Indians in becoming self-sufficient.

Mc Laughlin School

1890 – December 15. The rise of the Ghost Dance religion was making Indian agents uncomfortable, and McLaughlin mistakenly thought Sitting Bull was the leader of the movement. McLaughlin lobbied for Sitting Bull's arrest, and 43 agents broke into Sitting Bull's cabin in the Grand River area and took him at gunpoint. There is some confusion as to what happened next. By some accounts, there was a struggle, one of the agents was shot, and he in turn fatally shot Sitting Bull. Others say McLaughlin had given the order that Sitting Bull should be shot if he resisted arrest. Sitting Bull died and was buried at Fort Yates on the Standing Rock Reservation.

1895 – McLaughlin worked as a government inspector.

1923 – McLaughlin died at the age of 81.

Investigation

The high school, "Home of the Mighty Midgets," is claimed to be haunted according to the students and parents we spoke to. Most people said the deaths of the janitor and coach occurred a long time ago, and nobody could recall the names or the details of the deaths. Several people also told us about a series of haunted tunnels that run beneath the school.

We only had vague directions to the Historic McLaughlin House and spent several hours driving up and down the streets in search of it, with the assumption there would be a historical marker in the front yard. Eventually we went into a grocery store to ask for directions from the first person we met. His response was, "Of course I know where it is. It's my house." He doubted that the house was haunted and was emphatic that during all the years he lived there nothing strange had ever happened. He did, however, reluctantly concede that other people had visited his house and could sense that it was haunted.

Nobody we spoke to had heard of the headless ghost. We are still checking to see if there is any validity to this story.

We did find eyewitnesses who swear they saw the silhouette of the Devil standing on the top of Devil's Butte. It is not certain if the butte got its name based on the frequent sightings or if there is a connection.

At the Bear Soldier Bingo Hall, we spoke with Sterling, an employee who had worked at the bingo hall for well over four years. During that time he had never personally experienced anything that could not be explained. He said there is no truth to the story about the building being built on a cemetery. However, back in the 1960s, the trains would deliver the caskets of soldiers who were killed during the Vietnam War, and they were stored in this building because it was near the railroad tracks. Some believe the dead soldiers haunt the bingo hall.

Other people we spoke to reported a number of strange things. Doors would open and close on their own. Voices would be heard in the restroom. Sometimes a shout of "bingo!" would be heard by

McLaughlin House

everybody, but nobody in the room had a bingo on their card. It just seemed to be a disembodied voice coming from an indeterminate direction.

The other most commonly reported phenomenon is the unexplained movement of objects. People have had things like bingo cards, plates, and cups move. But other times larger things like tables and chairs will move. Nearly everybody in town knew about the haunting at the bingo hall and enthusiastically cited the evidence that has nearly the entire town convinced of a ghostly presence. A security guard for the bingo hall discovered he had inadvertently captured something supernatural on an overnight security camera. The video shows a chair moving back away from a table, then sliding clear across the room.

WESTERN SOUTH DAKOTA

Badlands National Park

Location: Badlands, South Dakota
Mailing Address: 25216 Ben Reifel Place, P.O. Box 6,
Interior, SD 57750-0006
Phone: (605) 433-5361 (Visitor Information)
Fax: (605) 433-5248
Website: www.nps.gov/badl

Directions: From Interstate-90 take the Badlands exit.

Ghost Lore

There are many places throughout the world that will make you feel
like you are from a different planet, but there are only a few places
that actually look like another planet. The Badlands are one such
place. Sprawling out over 240,000 acres of eroded buttes, spires,
and pinnacles, the Badlands will transport you back millions of
years. It is this unique landscape that continues to mesmerize mil-

lions of visitors each year. If you drive through the Badlands during the day, you may catch a glimpse of bison, the black-footed ferret, mule deer, sheep, or even some coyotes. However, if you venture through the Badlands at night, you may spot one of the many spirits still roaming the area.

- Strange ghostly noises can be heard while passing through the Badlands.

- Mysterious apparitions have been spotted in the area.

History

The Badlands contain Oligocene epoch fossil beds dating back 23-25 million years.

For over 11,000 years humans have lived in the Badlands area.

1890s – The Badlands were used for the Native American Ghost Dances.

1935 – The area that would later become the Badlands National Monument was chosen as a good site for the reintroduction of buffalo, pronghorn, and mountain sheep.

1939 – The Badlands National Monument was established.

1955 – The Millard family donated almost 19 acres of land in front of the Cedar Pass Lodge.

1956 – The National Park Service initiated a 10-year conservation development program. Approximately five million dollars was set aside for roads, buildings, and trails.

1957 – The boundaries of the Badlands National Monument were redefined.

1958 – The first full-time naturalist for the park was hired.

1959 – The visitor center that houses the park's headquarters, exhibits, and information was completed.

1963 – The first bison were released in Sage Creek Basin.

1964 – Bighorn sheep were re-introduced into the area.

1964 – The National Park Service purchased the Cedar Pass Lodge from the Millard Family for $275,000.

1978 – The Badlands were re-designated as the Badlands National Park.

Currently – The Badlands are one of South Dakota's most popular tourist destination.

Investigation

Stories of paranormal happenings have been in the Badlands area for hundreds of years. The *National Geographic Magazine* reported on Lakota legends that tell of the "Water Monsters of the Badlands." The legends state that the Badlands were the site of a war between the water spirits (*Unktehi*) and the thunder and lighting spirits (*Wakinyan*). It is said that the Wakinyan cast fire down on the Badlands to boil and dry up the sea. The remains of all the spirits can still be found in the area. It should be noted that paleontologists are still discovering bones of giant marine reptiles and giant flying reptiles from the Badlands.

Native Americans believe that the land is sacred. Many ghost dances were performed in the area in hopes of bringing back the dead.

Those traveling through the area report hearing the wails from the spirits of those who once lived in the area. Witnesses report that if one listens, they will hear the wind carrying the voices of the past.

Ruth Hein, in her book *Ghostly Tales of the Black Hills,* tells of visitors to the area hearing the strange wails of Native American spirits forever roaming the Badlands.

Crazy Horse Memorial

Location: Crazy Horse, Custer County, South Dakota
Address: Avenue of the Chiefs, Crazy Horse, SD 57730-9506
Phone: (605) 673-4681
Fax: (605) 673-2185
E-mail: memorial@crazyhorse.org
Website: www.crazyhorse.org

Directions: Follow 244 west past Mt. Rushmore to US 385.
Go south on 385 about 5 miles.

Ghost Lore

Carved out of the giant rock of the Black Hills, the Crazy Horse Memorial is a mind-boggling 563 feet in height and 641 feet in length. When completed, the memorial will be the largest sculpture in the world. The memorial was constructed in the spirit of Crazy Horse to show the white man that the red man has great heroes too. When asked by the white man "Where are your lands now?" Crazy

Horse replied, "My lands are where my dead lie buried." Although Crazy Horse is not buried at the memorial, many feel that his spirit calls the mountain home.

History

1842 – Many experts believe that Crazy Horse was born during this year.

1876 – Crazy Horse led his Oglala Sioux in the battle of Little Bighorn.

1877 – Under a truce, Crazy Horse was stabbed in the back by an American solider and passed away at the age of 35.

1939 – Korczak Ziólkowski was asked to assist Gutzon Borglum in sculpting Mt. Rushmore.

1948 – Ziólkowski, at the request of several Lakota Chiefs agreed to construct the Crazy Horse Memorial.

1982 – Ziólkowski passed away at the age of 74. He had worked on the memorial for nearly 36 years.

Currently – The memorial is a non-profit organization that looks to house the mountain carving, the Indian Museum of North America, and the Indian University and Medical Training Center of North America.

Investigation

In accordance to strong Native American beliefs, Crazy Horse resisted being photographed. The memorial is not an exact carving of Crazy Horse; it is more a symbol of his spirit.

Crazy Horse was widely known to have never signed a treaty or to have touched a pen.

We spoke with an employee of the memorial that reported that numerous visitors will come to the memorial not expecting anything paranormal to happen. Yet while they are there they will see the spirits of Native American ghosts at the memorial.

Ziólkowski always believed that the spirit of Crazy Horse resided at the memorial. Ziólkowski was certainly not alone as many visitors believe that the spirit of Crazy Horse is indeed still on the land he loved so much.

Those visiting the memorial will sense many spirits still lingering on the land. We spoke with several visitors who were overcome with emotion due to the spirits at the memorial. The witnesses spoke of the land being sacred and that it housed many spirits.

Staff told us of several accounts of visitors hearing the sounds of what they thought were the voices of those who had passed on. When told of these encounters, staff will tell the witnesses that they often hear similar reports from many other visitors of the memorial.

Those who get the opportunity to tour the actual mountain report feeling the sense of the sacredness of the mountain and being overwhelmed by the feeling of spirits around them.

The Black Hills Playhouse

Location: Custer, Custer County, South Dakota
Address: 24834 South Playhouse Road, Custer, SD 57730-8328
Mailing Address: P.O. Box 2513, Rapid City, SD 57709-2513
Phone: (605) 255-4141 or (605) 255-4551
Reservations: 1-800-636-0626
Email: BHPHQ@aol.com
Website: www.blackhillsplayhouse.com

Directions: From Highway 16A take 87. From 87 (Needles) turn onto Playhouse Road. The theatre will be straight ahead.

Ghost Lore

Tucked away, off the beaten path of the main road sits the historic Black Hills Playhouse. Surrounded by acres of pristine Black Hills Forest, the theatre brings a touch of culture to the welcoming wilderness. Yet, if you are not careful, you may unknowingly pass by the theatre altogether. However, if you are observant as you pass through the beautiful Black Hills, you may catch a glimpse of the numerous animals that live there. Those who are lucky and watchful may spot buffalo, deer, or a coyote. Those who are even luckier may spot the ghosts haunting the Black Hills Playhouse.

- Costumes will be laid out on their own.
- A former worker's daughter still haunts the place.
- Items reportedly move around by themselves.

History

1930s – The area housed Camp Lodge which was created by the Civilian Conservation Corps. This camp was designed as part of the federal relief program during the depression for men that were jobless. The men would work on creating State and National Parks including lakes, roads, campgrounds and bridges.

1940s – A Professor of Drama at the University of South Dakota, Warren "Doc" Lee wanted to create a theatre that would be set in the picturesque Black Hills of South Dakota.

1952 – Doc Lee served as the Dean of the College of Fine Arts until 1968.

1955 – The construction of the theatre was started and created much excitement in the area.

1968 – Lee became the Director of the Black Hills Fine Arts Center.

1975 – Professor Lee retired from the University of South Dakota.

1978 – Doc Lee passed away.

Currently – The Black Hills Playhouse is used to put on performances. The playhouse is associated with the University of South Dakota and the South Dakota Arts Council.

Investigation

The daughter of a former worker is said to haunt the old costume room. Many people believe that the woman is the daughter of a miner that worked for the Civilian Conservation Corps. Others believe that the ghost is actually one of the old workers and not the daughter.

Others associated with the playhouse believe that it is the ghost of Warren "Doc" Lee that continues to haunt the theatre he loved so much while he was alive.

Much of the haunting activity involves costumes being picked out by some unseen force. Often times, the workers will go home for the evening only to come back the next day and find that certain costumes have been picked out for the actors.

The Bullock Hotel

Location: Deadwood, Lawrence County, South Dakota
Official Name: The Bullock Hotel & Casino
Address: 633 Main Street, Deadwood, SD 57732-1123
Phone: (605) 578-1745
Fax: (605) 578-1382

Ghost Lore

A lot of travelers like to visit the various historic sites and buildings
of a town. Usually, every town has at least one or two historical
places hidden in them; unless, of course, that town is Deadwood.
You see, Deadwood does not just have one or two historical sites;
the whole town is listed as a historic landmark. Deadwood's history is overflowing with unique characters and one of most famous is
Seth Bullock. In addition to being a hardware store owner and
hotel proprietor, Bullock was Deadwood's first Sheriff. As Sheriff,
Bullock looked to bring some much needed order to the renegade

town. Bullock was known far and wide as an imposing man with an ice cold stare that even gained the respect of Deadwood's most unsavory characters. Those who knew him believed that he could outstare an angry cobra or a rogue elephant. If you are looking to stare down his grave, you can find it high up the hill in Mt. Moriah Cemetery. Yet if you don't want to hike to the top of the hill to stare at his grave, then you can check into his haunted Historic Bullock Hotel where you may have a chance to stare him down face-to-face.

- The hotel is haunted by the former owner who refuses to leave.

- The *Unsolved Mysteries* television program featured the hotel on one of their programs.

- Strange apparitions still linger throughout the hotel.

- Several of the rooms are said to be very haunted and guests have captured proof.

- Phantom footsteps have been heard walking throughout the hotel.

History

1884 – Seth Bullock met then-US Deputy Sheriff, Theodore Roosevelt. The two became good friends.

1890s – Roosevelt appointed Bullock to the position of first Forest Supervisor of the Black Hills.

1894 – Seth Bullock and his friend Sol Starr came to Deadwood and built a hardware store. Most of the store ended up destroyed by fire. Bullock became the first sheriff in Deadwood, and it became his mission to bring order to the outlaw town.

1895 – Seth constructed the Bullock Hotel. The three-story sixty-room hotel cost nearly forty-thousand dollars and took nearly two years to complete.

1896 – The hotel was completed and opened to an excited audience.

1900 – Bullock acquired a small building on the south end of the hotel. This addition is currently part of the hotel.

1905 – President Roosevelt appointed Bullock to the position of United States Marshall for the District of South Dakota.

1910 – President William Howard Taft reappointed Bullock to his position.

1913 – President Woodrow Wilson also reappointed Bullock to his position.

1919 – President Roosevelt passed away.

1919 – Bullock erected a monument to honor Roosevelt on Sheep Mountain.

1919 – Seth died of cancer in room 211 of the Bullock Hotel. His

body was buried in the Mt. Moriah Cemetery along with other famous Deadwood citizens Calamity Jane and Will Bill Hickok.

1976 – Many original items from the hotel were auctioned off when the Aryes Family sold the building.

1990s – The Historical Bullock Properties Group bought up several historical buildings in Deadwood. The goal of the group was to restore the buildings to their original splendor.

During renovation, the Bullock Hotel converted the over sixty rooms into twenty-eight rooms in order to make the rooms larger and more spacious.

Investigation

The hotel was featured on *Unsolved Mysteries*. The ghosts of the Bullock Hotel were showcased during a 1992 episode.

Guests staying in rooms 205, 207, 209, 211, 302, 305, and 314 have all reported paranormal activity.

Photo Courtesy of Arika Huck & the Bullock Hotel.

In the basement of the hotel sits Seth's Cellar Restaurant. The restaurant staff informed us that while they were working throughout the restaurant, they would hear the piano mysteriously play an old ragtime tune on its own. They believed that the ghosts of the hotel were upset that the restaurant had been moved.

Plates, glasses, and barstools from Seth's Cellar Restaurant are often seen being moved by some phantom force. We spoke with one patron who was amongst five other people who all witnessed a glass flying off the rack from above the bar and crashing on the floor. The bartender casually quipped that the ghost does this all the time. Many people believe that Seth's Cellar Restaurant is the most haunted location in the building.

Guests and staff report that the barstools in Bully's Bar will be moved by some unseen force. Even more bizarre are the reports that the chairs next to the bar's fireplace will often re-arrange themselves.

Several staff reported that they will be working throughout the hotel when they spot a ghost of a tall imposing man walking

Photo Courtesy of Arika Huck & the Bullock Hotel.

through the halls. Often times the ghost will disappear into thin air or will simply walk through a solid wall.

Several guests have reported that while relaxing in the hotel, they heard a ghostly male voice call out their name. Most were extremely baffled when they found no one else was around. Other guests report being tapped on the shoulder by unseen hands.

Staff informed us that many visitors request room 211 while staying at the hotel. Room 211 is the room in which Seth died. Those brave enough to spend the night in room 211 report seeing the ghostly apparition of Seth.

A guest told us that they were staying in the hotel for a vacation. They left the hotel for a while to go explore the historic town. Upon returning to the room, they were shocked to find that someone or something had moved all of their possessions around.

Often guests spending the night in one of the haunted rooms report that the room lights will turn off and on by themselves.

Photo Courtesy of Arika Huck & the Bullock Hotel.

We spoke with several maintenance staff who informed us that many times while working in the hotel, they would leave their cleaning carts directly outside of a room, but when they return the carts will have been moved. Although this phenomenon takes place quite often, staff have still not found a cause.

Both staff and guests have reported hearing the eerie sounds of phantom footsteps in the hallways of the hotel. Those brave enough to peek out of their rooms never seem to find the cause of these ghostly footsteps.

One man was staying at the hotel and had no idea of the haunting activity that has made the hotel famous. He was extremely puzzled when he saw the ghost of a tall man walking the hallway near his room. The guest reported that the ghost just disappeared right

before his eyes. After seeing a photo of Seth Bullock, the man was convinced that the ghost he had seen near his room was Seth.

Seth's ghost is actually quite a popular ghost, as it is one of the most frequently seen ghosts of the hotel. Many of the witnesses report coming face-to-face with the unmistakable ice cold stare that made Seth so feared and respected while he was alive.

The ghost of Seth Bullock also seems to appear when employees are taking a break or appear to be working at a slow pace. Many believe that even from the grave, Seth is trying to keep a watchful eye on his employees.

A couple and their seven-year-old grandchild were staying in room 306. The young child left the room in search of the vending machine. The child got twisted around and soon became lost. The grandfather was starting to get worried when he opened the door to go search for the child. Much to his surprise the child was standing right outside the door. The child explained that he had gotten lost and that someone had helped him find his way back to the room. The next day, while checking out of the hotel, the young boy pointed to a picture of Seth Bullock and exclaimed "Look, that's the nice man that helped me find my way back to the room!"

Seth's ghost is not the only spirit seen in the hotel as others have reported seeing the apparition of a young girl in the hotel. The girl is seen mostly in the basement where young children were kept during the typhoid fever and small pox outbreak in Deadwood.

Visitors to the casino often report catching the strong scent of roses and lilacs while on the casino floor. These mysterious smells often take place during the winter months when the natural smells of the flowers would be less likely. These smells are believed to be from the perfume of the lady ghost that roams the first and second floors.

Other ghostly smells of the hotel include a roaming cigar odor that lingers in places that no one has been in or smoked in.

Several perplexed guests have reported hearing the sounds of a woman weeping along with sounds of a crying child. However, much to their amazement, when they look out into the hallway no one is there and the eerie noises stop.

A cowboy staying at the hotel during the Days of '76 event was partaking in an afternoon nap when someone kept knocking at his door. Upset at the loss of his nap, the cowboy waited at the door for the perpetrator to strike again. When the knock came again, he opened his door and could see another cowboy standing out in the hallway. He flung open the door to catch the prankster, but was mystified when the cowboy he had just seen was not there. The man reported that someone then shoved him into the hallway and slammed the door behind him.

The radios in the hotel are often changed from a modern station to a country music station. This phenomenon is even reported when the radios are unplugged.

A woman staying in room 313 approached the front desk with her alarm clock. She reported that she had unplugged it because the light of the clock was keeping her awake. At approximately 2:30

a.m., the alarm clock went off by blasting country music. The woman was so spooked that she refused to allow the alarm back into her room.

Another guest of room 313 showed up at the front desk in her pajamas. This woman had awoken from her sleep to find a man in a cowboy hat standing at the foot of her bed. She was so shaken by the encounter that staff had to pack up her belongings because she refused to return to the room.

(Special thanks to Arika Huck and the Bullock Hotel for providing additional research and photos.)

The Green Door

Location: Deadwood, Lawrence County, South Dakota
Official Name: Wild West Winners Casino
Address: 622 Main Street, Deadwood, SD 57732-1111
Phone: (605) 578-1100
Toll Free: 1-888-880-3835

Ghost Lore

At one time Deadwood was famous for its brothels that operated openly, albeit illegally. Every year, during deer hunting season, the train would pull into town with scores of men who had convinced their wives they were on hunting trips, but were in fact after a prey of a different sort.

Although the houses of prostitution have long since been shut down, many believe the "ladies of the night" still haunt the night in the back rooms and dark corners of what used to be one of

Deadwood's most popular brothels--the Green Door.

During a cold winter in the 1920s, a prostitute had a baby and kept it hidden from the madam for fear of losing her job. One night a customer discovered the crying baby in the closet and killed it in front of the horrified mother. Today people can hear the ghostly infant crying upstairs.

Another version of the story is that a young prostitute was severely beaten by a customer and left to die in a closet. The ghostly sounds of her sobs can be heard coming from the closet.

- The closet is haunted by either a prostitute or a young child.

- People will close the closet door, but upon checking it later,

they find it has mysteriously reopened on its own.

- Hushed voices, laughter, and footsteps can sometimes be heard inside empty rooms. Other times people will hear either a young woman or a child crying.

- Other doors upstairs will open and close on their own, but most often, they will violently slam shut.

- Eyewitnesses have seen objects move.

- People commonly experience the feeling of being watched or the feeling that somebody is standing behind them when nobody is there.

- Phantom figures of "ladies of the evening" have been seen peering from the upstairs windows.

- Objects would be mysteriously moved or misplaced from the bar downstairs.

History

1897 – The original building was constructed for the Salvation Army. It was later destroyed by fire.

1903-1906 – The building that currently stands was constructed and used as a brothel.

1950s-1980 – Hazel "Dixie" Fletcher operated the Green Door brothel in Deadwood.

1980 – Federal law enforcement agents shut down the Green Door. Other brothels that were raided included the Purple Door, the Beige Door, and the White Door.

Investigation

The original building that was the Green Door is now a part of the Wild West Winners Casino. Employees report that most of the haunting activity occurs in the upstairs which is not open to the public and, unlike the rest of the building, has never been renovated. It looks just as it did when it served as a brothel in the early 1900s.

Employees report their uneasiness about these rooms from the past and confirm the reports of the mysterious slamming of the doors and other ghostly activity. Management discourages the employees from going upstairs, but one Halloween some of the workers secretly went up there and afterwards would only say that the frightening things they encountered were enough to convince them the place was haunted.

The second-story windows overlooking the street do have mannequins of the turn-of-the-century ladies of the evening. It is not certain if people have mistaken these for apparitions or if the sightings had occurred long before the mannequins were ever there.

It should be noted that although Saloon #10, where Wild Bill Hickok was killed, no longer stands, the Wild West Winners Casino is built on the original location. The original saloon was destroyed in a fire and relocated across the street.

Miss Kitty's

Location: Deadwood, Lawrence County, South Dakota
Official Name: Schnitzelz in Miss Kitty's Casino
Address: 649 Main Street, Deadwood SD 57732-1123
Phone: (605) 578-7778
Toll Free: 1-800-873-1876

Ghost Lore

Many of us complain about our jobs and dream of being in a different line of work, but could you imagine being trapped in an unwanted job even after death?

Claire was a former slave who worked as a cook at Miss Kitty's in Deadwood. What she really wanted to do was to be an artist. In her spare time, when she could afford the materials, the talented young black woman would brush paint onto canvases and create beautiful portraits, still lifes, and landscapes--artwork that nobody would see or appreciate.

Ultimately, her unfulfilled life ended tragically when she was murdered. After her death, she was quickly forgotten, but her frustrations with work and aspirations to be an artist lived on.

Most of the haunting activity centers around the Schnitzelz Restaurant in Miss Kitty's.

- An artist's paint brushes have materialized in the basement and various places in the building.

- A customer felt bristles brushing against her arm, looked down, and found a sable brush. Moments earlier nothing had been there.

- One employee felt her hair being touched and played with by unseen hands.

- Items would be mysteriously misplaced. Things would be lost and reappear the next day in another location. It's common for things to be mysteriously moved from the upstairs to the basement or vice-a-versa.

- Plates, silverware, and glasses will be moved or rearranged.

- One employee, fed up with the miscrievious pranks of the ghost, challenged Claire to show herself. At that moment a plate flew across the room and shattered against the wall. After that, no more challenges were issued.

History

Little is known about the history of the building, except that it was built around the 1900s and may have been a restaurant in the past.

The Schnitzelz Restaurant is a recent addition to Miss Kitty's Casino. The Schnitzelz chain was started in Canada by German immigrant Jack Niemann and features a unique German menu.

Investigation

Because the haunting activity was becoming more frequent, the staff decided to call in a psychic. It was the psychic who identified the ghost as Claire and determined that it was the presence of the restaurant that disturbed her.

Another center of spiritual activity is the basement under Miss Kitty's. This is the original cellar with a rock foundation and dirt floors. Most of the employees are too creeped out to even venture down there. It is not known why so much ghostly energy is concentrated in that spot. We could speculate that if Claire was a labor-

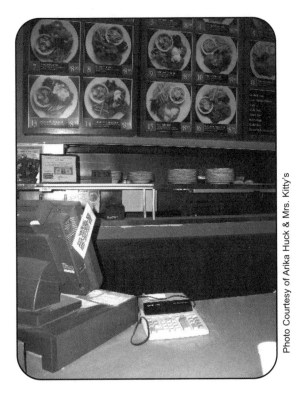

Photo Courtesy of Arika Huck & Mrs. Kitty's

Scene where the plate flew across the room.

Mount Moriah Cemetery

Location: Deadwood, Lawrence County, South Dakota
Phone: (605) 578-2600

Directions: From US 85 (Sherman St.) in Deadwood turn left on Cemetery St. (becomes Van Buren St.), turn left on Lincoln Ave. (become Jackson St.), enter cemetery parking lot.

Ghost Lore

Mount Moriah is without doubt the most famous cemetery in South Dakota, and many would even say it's the most haunted. Strange things have been reported here.

- A sense of being watched and followed while strolling through the cemetery.

- Feelings of unexplained fear and trepidation.

- Apparitions of phantoms wandering in the Chinese section.

- Moving shadows late at night.

History

1877 or 1878 – The Ingleside Cemetery was started in an area in Deadwood known as Whitewood Gulch. According to the Deadwood Cemetery Association, Rufus Wilsey was the first buried here. The *Black Hills Daily Times* maintains that it was James DeLong.

1878-1880 – About 350 infants and children died from an outbreak of diphtheria and scarlet fever and were buried in the cemetery.

1879 – As Deadwood rapidly grew, level ground became prime real estate for homes and businesses, so the town decided to move the cemetery to the top of a hill and rename it Mount Moriah cemetery. Because the grave markers were made of wood, many of them had deteriorated due to time and the weather; consequently, not all

of the graves were found and relocated. Occasionally, even to this day, bones and skeletons will be unearthed in the Ingleside area.

1938 – The Deadwood Cemetery Association turned the cemetery over to the city for lack of funds.

1999-2002 – The city of Deadwood spent $3.5 million on a cemetery restoration project that refurbished monuments, rebuilt walls, restored ironwork and masonry work. They repaired the streets, installed curbs, and paved roads. Landscaping work was done and a visitor center was constructed.

Investigation

Every year between 80,000 and 100,000 people visit the cemetery.

Records exist for 3,627 burials. Many of these people died from natural disasters such as floods and fires, some died from accidents, and others were victims of murder. Other causes of death listed by the Deadwood Cemetery Association included:

Childbirth, "bad whiskey" (a euphemism for alcoholism), opium, catarrh, dropsy of the heart, summer complaint, softening of the brain, inflammation of the bowels, want of vitality, "God knows," killed by Indians, teething, old age, hobnail liver (cirrhosis), broken thumb, struck with bar glass, hanged by vigilantes, and from eating 14 hard-boiled eggs.

Many of the Chinese who worked in the mines had guarantees written in their labor contracts that within 10 years after their death their bones would be disinterred and shipped back to China. They believed that if they were not properly buried on Chinese soil, their ghosts would eternally wander the earth. Unfortunately, many of the remains were not exhumed, and they remained buried in unmarked graves at Mount Moriah. Some visitors to the cemetery claim to have seen the spirits of these Chinese workers wandering through the graveyard late at night, unable to find eternal rest.

We spoke with two young employees of the cemetery who told us of their bizarre encounters while working there. The girls stated that while preparing to close the cemetery, they often would walk

through to make sure no one was left inside. While strolling past gravestones the girls would often catch a glimpse of a shadowy figure roaming the cemetery. However, the employees could never track this figure down.

We spoke with one employee who was convinced of the cemetery ghosts. She reported that during the evening while walking through the cemetery closing the gates, she would turn around to find that someone or something had mysteriously reopened the very same gates she had just closed.

Employees told us that while closing up in the gift shop, they would often hear strange noises coming from the cemetery. Upon listening closer, they would hear what sounded like mysterious voices engaged in conversation within the cemetery. Concerned that visitors might still be in the cemetery they would go to investigate, yet every time they went to check it out, they found the cemetery completely empty.

So much paranormal activity has taken place at the cemetery that several employees told us that they did not want to work alone due to fear.

**Famous Graves in
Mount Moriah Cemetery**

James Butler Hickok ("Wild Bill")
b. May 27, 1837
d. August 2, 1876

Wild Bill was born in Troy Grove, Illinois. He left home at age 18 to be a stagecoach driver on the Santa Fe and Oregon Trails. Because of his gun-fighting abilities, he acquired his nickname. In 1857, Wild Bill bought land in Kansas and became a con-stable. He became a constable in Nebraska in 1861, and his reputation as a gunfighter grew. In the Civil War, he served as a Union scout. After the war, Wild Bill became a US Deputy Marshal at Fort Riley in Kansas and at Abilene, Texas. When he accidental-ly shot and killed his own deputy, his days as a law man came to an end. He toured with Buffalo Bill Cody's Wild West Show from 1872 to 1873, then settled in Deadwood. He was assassinated by Jack "Broken Nose" McCall while playing poker at the #10 Saloon. The hand he was holding consisted of a pair of aces and a pair of eights, with all cards black. This has since been known as the "dead man's hand."

Virtually the entire town attended the funeral of Wild Bill Hickok. He was originally buried in Ingleside Cemetery, but at Calamity's request, in 1879, he was reinterred in Mount Moriah Cemetery.

The fence around Wild Bill's statue is over 100 years old. The current bust was created by David Young, and dedicated on Aug 02, 2002.

Seth Bullock
b. July 23, 1847
d. September, 1919

Seth Bullock was born in Canada. At the age of 16, he ran away from home and moved to Montana. In 1871 and 1872, he was elected to the Territorial Senate. During that time, he helped create Yellowstone National Park. In 1873, Bullock was elected Sheriff of Lewis and Clark County. He moved to Deadwood in 1876 to open a hardware store. After Wild Bill Hickok was shot and killed, Bullock was appointed sheriff of Deadwood, but never had to kill anybody. In 1884, he became a US Deputy Marshal, and at this time met Theodore Roosevelt, then a deputy US Deputy Sheriff from North Dakota. The two became lifelong friends. In 1894, his hardware store burned down. The following year, he built the Bullock Hotel, which continues to operate to this day. Bullock volunteered for active duty during the Spanish-American War in 1898, and was the Captain of Troop A in Grigsby's Cowboy Regiment of Theodore Roosevelt's Rough Riders. He was promoted to Captain Bullock. When Roosevelt became Vice President, he appointed Bullock as the first Forest Supervisor of the Black Hills Reserve. After Roosevelt was elected President, Bullock rode in the inaugural parade. After Roosevelt died, Bullock erected a monument to him on Sheep Mountain, renamed Mount Roosevelt.

Bullock died of cancer in room 211 of his own hotel and was buried at the top of the hill in Mount Moriah Cemetery. Mount Roosevelt can be seen from Bullock's grave.

Martha Jane Cannary ("Calamity Jane")
b. May 1, 1852
d. August 1, 1903

Martha Jane Cannary was born in Missouri. Her parents died when she was young. She served as an army scout with Custer, and fought in several military conflicts with Native Americans and acquired the nickname "Calamity Jane" in 1872, after rescuing her commanding officer, Captain Egan. Eagan was shot during an ambush, and she threw him onto her horse and rode with him back to the fort. In 1876, Calamity Jane moved to Deadwood and became close friends with Wild Bill Hickok and Charlie Utter. She told people she was briefly married to Wild Bill and that he fathered her child, but the claim is doubtful. During the smallpox epidemic, Calamity Jane was apparently immune and helped to care for the sick and dying. In 1884, she moved to El Paso, Texas and married

Clinton Burke the following year. She gave birth to a daughter in 1876, but by 1895 the marriage with Burke was over. In 1896, she toured with the Wild West shows and did this until she died from complications of pneumonia in 1903.

In accordance with her dying request, she was buried in Mount Moriah Cemetery next to Wild Bill Hickok.

John E. Perrett ("Potato Creek Johnny")
b. 1866
d. February 26, 1943

John E. Perrett was born in Wales, but immigrated to the Dakota Territory in 1883 at the age of 17. He worked a variety of odd jobs, eventually becoming a prospector.

He gained his nickname by staking his claim on Potato Creek and gained fame in 1929 when he found what was purported the largest gold nugget in the Black Hills. Later, he sold the 7 ¾ troy ounce nugget to the Adams Museum, and they currently have a replica on display. Potato Creek Johnny, a diminutive man, was only 4 feet 3 inches tall. As he got older and let his whiskers grow longer, he looked like the classic old-time prospector. He was one of Deadwood's most colorful characters, and people would come from miles around to have their picture taken with him or just to watch him prospecting at Potato Creek.

He died at age 77 and was buried next to Wild Bill Hickok and Calamity Jane.

Henry Weston Smith ("Preacher Smith")
b. January 10, 1827
d. August 20, 1876

Henry Weston Smith was born in Ellington, Connecticut. He was an ordained Methodist minister who served in the Civil War, and later became a doctor. He moved to Kentucky, then to Dakota Territory to do missionary work. In 1876, he settled in Deadwood and was the first and only preacher there. He preached on Sundays and worked odd jobs during the week. One Sunday morning, he posted a note on the door of his cabin indicating he had gone to Crook City to preach a sermon, but he never returned. Later a rancher found the body of Preacher Smith on the road about three miles northwest of Deadwood. Indians were blamed for his death, but many suspected he was killed by people concerned he might disrupt the local economy by drawing away customers from business establishments that provided drinking, gambling, and prostitution.

Preacher Smith was buried in Ingleside Cemetery, but reinterred when the cemetery was moved to Mount Moriah.

1880 Train

Location: Hill City, Pennington County, South Dakota
Mailing Address: 1880 Train, Box 1880, Hill City, SD 57745-1880
Address: Black Hills Central Railroad 1880 Train, 222 Railroad Avenue, Hill City, SD 57745-1880
Phone: (605) 574-2222
Fax: (605) 574-4915
Email: office@1880train.com
Website: www.1880train.com
Directions: Hill City Depot between East Main Street & Elm Street.

Ghost Lore

Ghosts seem to have a fascination with the railroads. Perhaps the spirits have fond memories of having spent long hours riding the trains, and they would prefer to hang out there after death.

In Hill City there is an old dining car that has been converted into a tourist restaurant known as The Highliner Eatery. Customers have seen a strange man sitting in the back of the room. According to descriptions, he is dressed in a brown suit of a style worn in the 1880s. Upon approaching the man, people say he vanishes before their eyes.

History

In 1880, CB&Q Railroad Company provided train service for the workers in the mines and mills between Hill City and Keystone.

Today the 1880 vintage steam train with Old Baldwin engines and 19th-century coaches takes tourists on a two-hour narrated round trip through the Black Hills.

Investigation

The owner of the eatery is uncertain that the place is haunted, but acknowledged that her brother was one of the eyewitnesses who saw the phantom in the dining car.

Alpine Inn

Location: Hill City, Pennington County, South Dakota
Mailing Address: P.O. Box 211, Hill City, SD 57745-0211
Address: 225 Main Street, Hill City, SD 57745
Phone: (605) 574-2749

Ghost Lore

Although some people consider hauntings to be a bad thing and will even seek out ghostbusters to exorcise the spirits from their premises, others consider the hauntings to be a positive thing. Such is the case at the historic Alpine Inn.

The owner and employees of this restaurant have all experienced the typical signs of haunting activity. Lights turn on and off; voices and footsteps can be heard. However, instead of creating fear, these spirits create a feeling of comfort and security.

History

1886 – The historic building on Main Street was constructed as a motel.

1986 – The Alpine Inn was converted into a Bavarian-themed gift shop and restaurant.

Investigation

The owner does not like to use the words "ghosts" or "haunted," but she does confirm that she shares her dwelling with "protective spirits."

These spirits do like to make their presence known, and people have heard unexplained footsteps and voices, particularly on the second floor, where the owner used to live. She says that on more than one occasion she woke up to find the spirits standing over her, apparently watching her while she slept to make sure she was safe. Her daughter had also reported similar experiences while sleeping there.

Apparently, even their dog could sense the presence of these spirits and would react whenever they were near.

As evidence that the spirits protect the building, she cited an occasion when Hill City was hit by a damaging hail storm. While the hail bombarded all the surrounding businesses, the Alpine Inn remained unscathed.

The owner had long suspected that one of these guardian spirits was a dear friend of hers who had passed away several years ago. She feels that her suspicions were eventually confirmed when a psychic woman came to the restaurant and asked her if she had ever known a woman by the name of "Bernice Muschamp" because she could sense her presence at the inn. This happened to be the name of the owner's dead friend.

A Dakota Dream

Location: Hot Springs, Fall River County, South Dakota
Address: A Dakota Dream, 801 Almond Street, Hot Springs, SD 57747-1301
Phone: (605) 745-4633
Toll Free: (888) 881-4633
Email: villa@gwtc.net
Website: www.blackhillsguesthouse.com

Directions: From US-385 (SR-87) turn West onto Summit Road. From Summit turn South onto Almond Street. Arrive at A Dakota Dream.

Ghost Lore

Perched high above the historic downtown of Hot Springs, this elegant eight-bedroom B&B provides visitors with a chance to get away from their busy lives and spend some time by themselves. However, many visitors report that they are joined by guests that have never checked out.

- The home is said to be haunted by a former owner who refuses to leave.

- Doors in the home open and close seemingly on their own.

- Strange apparitions have been sighted by both the owners and guests.

- Mysterious unexplained smells have been detected in the home.

History

1891 – Developer Fred Evans constructed a spa retreat with the hope that it would be a vacation spot for the tired wealthy tourists in town to partake in the natural hot springs.

1916 – The Spanish Style home Villa Theresa was constructed near the spa by Ernest DeMoulin.

1925 – Chicago businessman and multimillionaire F.O. Butler purchased Fred Evan's home. The home was used for high roller getaways.

1926 – F.O. Butler had the house renovated by Marshall Fields.

1955 – F.O. Butler passed away.

1974 – The Akhtar family purchased the guest house. The family used it as their residence for several years.

1980 – The home was used for a private residence. A lot of activity was said to be caused by the renovation.

1990 – Margaret and Dick Hunter purchased the Villa Theresa. The Hunters planned to renovate the historic home into a B&B.

Currently – The home is owned by Richard and Deborah Henderson.

Investigation

Many current books and articles incorrectly refer to the home by its old names of Villa Theresa Guest House or the Toal House.

The original home was not quite as squeaky clean as some would have thought. Many in the Hot Springs area knew of it as a place to go drink, gamble, and enjoy the "ladies of the night" that worked there. It should be noted that this was not unusual for the time period.

A former owner reported that while she was relaxing in the living room, she noticed an extremely attractive woman walk down the stairs. The mysterious woman was said to be wearing an evening gown that appeared to be from the late 1800s. This mysterious

woman just disappeared into thin air.

Several guests were relaxing in the living room when they caught a glimpse of a ghost of a man standing by the fireplace smoking a cigar.

Newlyweds were at the home for their honeymoon. The wife decided to take a shower, while in the shower she heard a male voice saying extremely lewd things to her. She quickly jumped out of the shower and asked her husband if he had been talking to her. The wife was shocked when she noticed that he had been packing and had no idea what she was talking about.

A man taking a shower in the Rose Room, came out to find his room filled with the scent of a flowery perfume that was not there earlier.

In the Windows Room, a guest reported feeling that something was laying on her legs even though no one else was in the room.

The owner was busy cleaning in the basement when he heard his wife come down the stairs. He felt her pat him on the back, yet much to his surprise, when he turned around he found that no one was there.

Psychics visiting the home report seeing the spirits of two women. Both women are said to be dressed in Victorian-era clothing while one of the women is a blond, the other is a brunette.

In the Treasure Room a young man reported that he felt someone sit down on the bed next to him. He was surprised to find that no one was in the room with him. Other guests staying in the Treasure Room report that the door will often open and close on its own.

The current owner told us that a guest was staying in one of the rooms of the house that is equipped with its own entrance. During the evening the man witnessed the door handle moving back and forth as though someone was trying to enter. Thinking that some-one was playing a trick on him, the man quickly opened the door to

Mountain View Cemetery

Location: Keystone, Pennington County, South Dakota
Mailing Address: Mountain View Cemetery, 1901 Mountain View Road, Rapid City, SD 57702-4365
Phone: (605) 394-4189

Directions: From Cty Rd. 40 in Keystone, go south on Hwy 16 (Iron Mountain Rd.), and turn left on Cemetery Rd. Continue to the cemetery.

Ghost Lore

When traveling across South Dakota and staying at motels and hotels, most of us prefer a room with a view, but some people buried in South Dakota would prefer a grave with a view.

Mountain View Cemetery, hidden away in the back corner of Keystone, offers a clear view of Mount Rushmore in the distance. Many of the workers who assisted Gutzon Borglum in carving the monument are buried on this gently sloping hillside.

Some believe that on the darkest nights, when the National Memorial officials illuminate Mount Rushmore, the dead workers will rise up from their graves to gaze upon their work with pride.

There are also stories that the ghost of a prospector and his phantom burro haunt the cemetery at night. It is said that in life his attempts to find gold usually resulted in failure and disappointment. Undeterred, he continues his search for gold even into the afterlife.

History

Many of the Mount Rushmore workers and miners are buried in this cemetery.

Famous prospector, Harry "Wild Horse" Hardin (1896-1984), one of Keystone's more colorful characters, is buried here. He never made it rich as a prospector, but, in his later years, he was able to make a living posing for tourists with his burro, "Sugar Babe." Because he looked like the classic stereotype of an old prospector,

the Landstrom's Black Hills Gold Company in Keystone used his likeness for their logo. He died at the age of 88.

Investigation

The first thing we noticed upon entering this graveyard was a misspelling on the sign. "Cemetery" was spelled as "cemetary." The second thing we noticed was that virtually every grave was unique and personalized by family members and loved ones. Instead of using plastic flowers, people left coins, stones, toys, and other items that would have had meaning to the deceased. The third thing that caught our attention was the fact that the cemetery does indeed overlook Mount Rushmore.

Some investigators have reportedly captured white, ghostly faces and ethereal figures on film and videotape in the cemetery, and many of the people who have visited this place have left convinced that it is haunted. However, a few people vehemently reject a belief in ghosts and the afterlife. "Wild Horse" Harry would have countered with his favorite saying, "Everyone's got to believe in something." Hopefully he did not conclude that expression with, "I believe I'll have another beer."

Homestake Opera House

Location: Lead, Lawrence County, South Dakota
Address: 309 South Main Street, Lead SD 57754-1824
Phone: (605) 584-2067
Email: opera@leadoperahouse.org
Website: www.leadoperahouse.org

Directions: The theatre is right on Main Street in downtown Lead.

Ghost Lore

This elegant theatre, quietly nestled on Main Street, has been a part of Lead's history for over 90 years. During this time, numerous touring groups, community shows, and events have come and gone. However, many people believe that the one thing that has not left the theatre is the ghost.

- Doors mysteriously open and close on their own.

- The light and sound equipment often malfunction for no apparent reason.

- Strange cold breezes can be felt throughout the theatre.

History

1874 – Thomas Carey told his fellow miners that the gold was even better across the divide and many rushed to the camp which was known as Washington.

1876 – The town continued to grow and was famous for its large gold mine called the Homestake Mine.

1880 – The town of Lead was listed by the US Census. The population was listed at 1,440.

1894 – The widow of California Senator George Hearst, Phoebe Hearst, donated a library and established a kindergarten in Lead.

1911 – Phoebe Hearst brought the idea of the Homestake Opera House and Recreation Building to the Superintendent of the Homestake Mine, Mr. Thomas Grier. Together, they presented the idea to the citizens of Lead as a gift from Homestake. In addition to an opera house, the original plans called for a swimming pool, library, bowling alley, and social room.

1911 – The Homestake Recreation Center and Opera House project was officially announced to the public. Immediately there was much anticipation for the new project.

1912 – Workers began construction on the community project.

1914 – The Opera House opened its doors to an excited public. Over 1,000 people from Lead, Deadwood, and other surrounding towns came to see the first show.

1914 – Opera House co-founder Thomas Grier passed away.

1918 – The Opera House closed down due to a Spanish influenza outbreak. The town converted the Recreation Center into an emergency hospital.

1919 – The Opera House and Recreation Center opened once again.

1984 – A fire damaged the Opera House.

1997 – Historic Homestake Opera House Society was founded to preserve and restore the theatre.

2006 – With the help of a Save America's Treasures grant, the historic Opera House has been restored to its original glory.

Investigation

The theatre is known as the Jewel of the Black Hills.

We spoke with the current owner, who while rebuilding the theatre, had not had any paranormal experiences. The owner was familiar with the stories, but did not have any of his own.

The *Rapid City Journal* reported that the employees named the ghost of the theatre "Eric." The reasoning behind the name is not known.

The *Journal* also reported that a projectionist felt the presence of something unseen pass by him on the stairs.

Employees reported having difficulties with the theatre's equipment including both the sound and light equipment. The equipment would inexplicably malfunction during movies. No source for the malfunctioning was discovered.

Unexplainable electrical problems have been reported throughout the theatre.

YMCA

Location: Lead, Lawrence County, South Dakota
Official Name: Northern Hills Family YMCA
Address: 845 Miners Avenue, Lead, SD 57754
Phone: (605) 584-1113

Ghost Lore

Perhaps the appropriate background music for this story would be jazz pianist Jack Perla's "Swimming Lessons For The Dead." The YMCA in Lead is said to be haunted by a phantom swimmer who enjoys using the pool after-hours. We can only assume he was doing the dead-man's float.

History

1989 – The YMCA facility was constructed on what was a vacant lot. Among other things, it featured a six-lane, 25-yard pool, kids' wading pool, whirlpool, and sauna. Naturally, the programs offered included swimming lessons.

Investigation

A former employee came to work early in the morning and was the only person in the building. Looking into the pool area, he noticed a movement and disturbance in the water as if some invisible entity had swam the length of the pool. Normally the water was perfectly still, so he was justifiably suspicious that somebody else was in the building. Upon closer inspection, he discovered wet footprints, on the tiled floor, leading away from the pool. He began following the footprints, thinking they would direct him to the unauthorized swimmer, but was shocked to find they stopped mid-stride just a few feet from the pool, and nobody was to be found.

What was it that created the wake in the pool and the footprints? Most people are convinced that it was a ghost out for a morning swim. We found no evidence that anybody had ever died in this building.

People who were involved in the original construction of the YMCA told us it was built on a vacant lot, and, as far as they knew, there were never any homes or buildings constructed on this site previously.

After the discovery of gold in the 1870s, a mining camp was established in this area, and it is possible there were unmarked graves or forgotten cemeteries on this site that could account for the haunting.

Hotel Alex Johnson

Location: Rapid City, Pennington County, South Dakota
Address: 523 Sixth Street, Rapid City, SD 57701-2725
Phone: (605) 342-1210
Toll Free: 1-800-888-ALEX(2539)
Email: Info@AlexJohnson.com
Website: www.alexjohnson.com

Directions: From US-16 take the Main Street exit. Turn onto 6th Street and arrive at the hotel.

Ghost Lore

Whether it is through a movie, book, or TV show, most people like to experience ghosts from a distance. However, there is a large segment of the population that seeks a more personal encounter with these phantoms. If you are this type of person, then you may want to make your reservation at the historical Alex Johnson Hotel. The landmark hotel overlooking downtown Rapid City prides itself on being such a unique hotel that numerous guests continue to return, even those who are dead.

- Haunted by a former manager who jumped to her death.

- The elevators stop on their own without human intervention.

- Many of the staff report seeing spirits wandering through the hallways.

- Hotel instruments often mysteriously start up on their own.

- The hotel is built on the graves of children.

History

1927 – Alex Carlton Johnson began construction on a 10-story hotel one day before the first blasting of Mount Rushmore took place. Mr. Johnson served as the Vice President of the Chicago-Northwestern Railroad.

1928 – The 10-story hotel was constructed by Alex Carlton Johnson and opened to much anticipation within the community. He built the hotel as a tribute to the Native Americans of South Dakota. The hotel was dubbed "The Showplace of the West." The first registered guest was a Patsy O'Neill.

1933 – Johnson was given the honor of a Native American name of "Chief Red Star." Johnson was also made an honorary blood brother of Chief Iron Horse.

1936 – Franklin Delano Roosevelt stayed at the hotel during his tour through the West.

1938 – Alex Johnson passed away.

1981 – The hotel was listed on the National Register of Historic Places.

1980-2000s – Interior and exterior renovations took place in the hotel. Using photographs of the hotel from the 1920s, the renovations sought to recreate the same Lakota themes that Alex Johnson had constructed over 70 years ago.

Investigation

We found no evidence that the hotel was built on any graves, children or otherwise.

Room 812 is believed to be haunted by a woman who plunged to her death from the room. The *Rapid City Weekly News* reported that

a woman had indeed fallen to her death from the room in the 1970s. However, the woman was not the former manager that many people believe fell to her death.

We spoke with employees of the hotel who informed us that they believe Alex Johnson still haunts the hotel that he created. Many of the staff had personal stories of strange activity taking place in the hotel.

Many guests and staff report that the hotel elevator inexplicably stops on its own when it reaches the third floor. It is not known why the elevator stops on the third floor more than any other floor.

Staff have also reported hearing the sounds of faint cries from children while working on the third floor.

Several employees refuse to enter the eighth floor because of the ghostly activity. It was on the eighth floor that three employees suddenly got sick for no apparent reason.

A housekeeper reported seeing a ghost of a lady watching her as she worked. The employee reported that the ghost was strangely dressed. When looking at old photographs of the hotel, the woman discovered that the ghost she had seen was dressed in the same clothes as a 1920s maid. The witness was convinced that she had seen the ghost of a former maid that worked at the hotel.

Employees spoke of a young couple that stayed in room 802 with their pets. Upon entering their room, the pets were immediately agitated and were behaving strangely. The couple went to bed for the evening only to be woken up in the middle of the night to what sounded like music in the room. Although they were convinced that they had indeed heard music, no source could be found. The woman awoke again shortly after the music incident with the over-whelming feeling that some unseen force was trying to strangle her. Determined not to let the events of the previous evening ruin their plans, the couple spent another night in the same room. This time the husband woke up to the feeling of being choked. Needless to say the couple was extremely spooked when they noticed that the choking took place at the exact same time that the woman had been chocking the previous night.

A night security worker reported on several occasions that he had seen a strange ghostly figure walking the hallways of the hotel.

Staff working at the hotel report that the piano in the ballroom plays when no one is present. Visitors often hear the piano in the ball-room playing only to walk in and find the ballroom completely empty. However, the ballroom is not the only place people hear the piano being played, as others report hearing the piano throughout the hotel.

Hooky Jack's

Location: Rapid City, Pennington County, South Dakota
Address: 321 Seventh Street, Rapid City, SD 57701-2701
Website: www.phattymcgees.com/hooky_files/index.htm

Directions: From Main Street turn onto 7th Street and arrive at the restaurant.

Ghost Lore

As you walk through the historic downtown of Rapid City, you get the feel of what the city was like a hundred years ago. When you get to the building that Hooky Jack's restaurant is in, you actually are looking what the city looked like during the late 1880s. The old brick building provides you with a rare opportunity to see the history of the city first hand. However, as you enter the building, history may not be the only thing you experience first hand.

Built in the late 1880s, the building is said to be the oldest building in Rapid City.

- Strange footsteps have been reported throughout the restaurant.

- Chairs and other items in the restaurant move around on their own.

- The security cameras pick up unexplained lights in the restaurant.

History

1882 – A local miner named John Leary was rolling two sticks of dynamite in order to warm them for use in the mine. Unfortunately the dynamite was unstable and went off. Barely surviving the explosion, John lost both his forearms just above his elbows. John also lost his hearing in one ear and the sight in one of his eyes. John was fitted with two hooks to serve as his arms. His new arms served as the catalyst for the nickname Hooky Jack.

1883 – Unable to continue working in the mines, Hooky applied for a night security position of constable for Rapid City. It would be Hooky's job for the next 44 years.

1903 – The city records show the building was constructed to be used as a grocery wholesaler.

1900s – Throughout the early 1900s the building housed B.H. Grocer Wholesale Company.

1926 – Hooky died at the age of 77. He was struck by a vehicle

while crossing Main Street. The mayor of Rapid City issued a proclamation for Hooky's funeral. Most of the businesses in downtown closed in order to attend the funeral.

The building was home to several businesses before it became Hooky Jack's, including a cannery and furniture store.

2001 – Hooky Jack's restaurant opened.

Investigation

Employees will be working at the restaurant when they hear strange noises echoing throughout the building. Much to their surprise, the source of the sounds is never discovered.

Employees stack up the dining chairs at the end of the night. These stacks of chairs will often fall over as though they have been pushed by some unseen force.

Employees will be working throughout the restaurant when they notice items have been moved around without the aid of a fellow worker.

Many female employees refuse to go upstairs on their own during the evening because of the paranormal happenings that take place there.

Although no visual apparitions have been sighted, several of the bartenders get cold chills when they are working as though they are picking up on unseen spirits in the restaurant.

The owner informed us that the restaurant's surveillance cameras will often pick up strange orbs on the film. The camera often picks up other strange phenomena throughout the restaurant. Although the staff is baffled by these "orbs" no one has spotted them with their own eyes.

Moonshine Gulch and the Town of Rochford

Location: Rochford, Pennington County, South Dakota
Address: Moonshine Gulch Saloon, 22635 North Rochford Road, Rochford, SD 57745-6007
Phone: (605) 584-2743

Directions: From Highway 85, take the Rochford exit. The Gulch is on the only main road.

Ghost Lore

Positioned between Hill City and Deadwood, the Moonshine Gulch and town of Rochford get overrun with visitors looking to get a glimpse at the historic town. Once a bustling mining town, the town is now just a small dot on the map and an out of the way destination for the adventurous. However, those brave enough to look around this historic town often report experiencing the town's history first hand.

- Haunted by former miners of the area.
- Ghostly noises have been reported in the area.
- Employees of the bar encounter mysterious ghosts.
- The bar is haunted by a former owner.

History

1877 – The town of Rochford was founded by R.B. Hughes and M.D. Rochford.

1870s – The saloon opened during the Black Hills gold rush.

1878 – Rochford had a population of over 500.

1900 – The mining of the town had been unsuccessful and the town shrank down to 48 residents and a post office.

1910 – The Moonshine Gulch opened. It is thought that the building housed a saloon even before the Gulch.

Allie Hanen owned and operated the tavern before it was taken over by the Harns.

Currently – The Gulch is owned by the Harns.

Currently – The only businesses in Rochford are the Moonshine Gulch and the Rochford Mall.

Investigation

We spoke with the owner, Betsy Harn, who informed us that she believes that the place is haunted by the building's former owner Allie Hanen.

It is believed that Allie's grave is under the house. The owners did find a tombstone that they believed was Allie's. The tombstone is now buried under part of the building.

Often times the tavern's lights will not work.

Many items in the tavern will fall for no apparent reason. When these items fall, most witnesses blame it on the ghost.

Several of the staff have felt the presence of a male ghost in the tavern. Although many visitors and staff have not actually seen the ghost, most feel certain that he is there.

While working in the back hallway many employees have felt someone brush by them, even though no one was there.

We spoke with several residents who reported hearing what sounded like miners continuing to work in the woods.

Many in the town have had their own personal paranormal experience while spending time in the Gulch. Most speak of it in passing as though it was common place.

Visitors report seeing what appears to be the ghosts of former miners of the area.

In her book, *Tales of the Black Hills*, Helen Rezatta wrote that hunters have reported hearing the ghostly howls of frustrated claim jumpers throughout the area.

Gas Light Inn and Saloon

Location: Rockerville, Pennington County, South Dakota
Address: 13490 Main Street, Rockerville, SD 57702-7408
Phone: (605) 343-9276
Fax: (605) 343-1220
Website: www.thegaslightrestaurant.com

Directions: From US-16 take the Rockerville exit. The Gas Light is on the only main road.

Ghost Lore

Ghost Towns are towns that were once bustling with life. Often times these towns would quickly spring up around the discovery of gold within the area. Unfortunately, many of these ghost towns have died out and are now empty. However, even if the ghost town of Rockerville is not currently a booming place, it may actually have real ghosts.

- The saloon is haunted by the original owner of the Hotel Harney.

- Mysterious cold drafts have been felt by staff.

- Bottles unexplainably fall from the bar.

- A ghost often greets people coming into the bar.

History

1876 – Gold was discovered in the area by William Keeler and Rockville sprung up as a roaring mining camp.

1879 – A petition signed by the residents was sent to the postal authorities. The petition requested that the name of the town be changed from Rockville to Rockerville.

1880 – The population of the town was listed at over 1,000.

1920s or 30s – It is believed that the building was constructed in this time period, although no specific date has been confirmed.

1930 – With the end of the gold rush, the town of Rockerville was nearly deserted.

1950 – The town attempted to rebuild and reinvent itself as a tourist town.

1970 – When the new highway was built outside of Rockerville, the town lost favor with visitors and was once again abandoned.

1970s – The town was put up for sale during an auction.

1976 – The historic Hotel Harney in Rapid City was demolished.

The back bar, counter, and foot rail were brought into the inn's saloon.

1989 – The Gas Light was purchased by Dennis Kling and Westly Parker. The two set about restoring the building.

2002 – Keith Brink and Steve Zwetzig purchased the building.

2005 – Zwetzig bought out Brink and is the sole owner.

Investigation

Several staff believe the ghost of Samuelson Harney continues to haunt the place. Harney constructed the Harney Hotel in Rapid City where the bar was moved from. However, it should be noted that the old bar has since been sold and is no longer in the Gas Light.

Several visitors have seen a good-looking man standing by the door. Witnesses told us that the distinguished looking ghost is tall, thin, and well-dressed. Often times visitors see the man in the old

glass doors of the entrance. It looks as though the man is there to greet visitors as they enter the establishment.

We spoke with several staff who have seen the well-dressed man as they walked by the entrance.

Staff and visitors will feel a cold breeze go by them and when they look up, they see the ghost of the man in front of them.

Staff also reported to us that many times they will leave the room for a moment, and when they return, someone has turned on the faucet and left it running.

The children of a former owner also saw the ghost of the man. They reported that the ghost was nearly transparent as they could almost see right through him.

Most of the people who have seen the ghost state that he is a friendly ghost.

Numerous bartenders and workers have seen the ghost throughout the years. Reports of the ghost have been circulating for many years. We spoke with one employee that sighted the ghost 12 years ago.

During the Sturgis motorcycle rally, a couple was seated at the bar when a beer bottle fell off the bar, hit the cooler sideways, and landed back in the upright position. Those who witnessed the bottle's unusual landing were convinced that it was related to the ghost.

Bear Butte State Park

Location: Sturgis, Meade County, South Dakota
Mailing Address: P.O. Box 688, Sturgis, SD 57785-0688
Phone: (605) 347-5240
Fax: (605) 347-7627
Email: BearButte@state.sd.us

Directions: From Sturgis take Highway 79 north for approximately six miles. There you will see the entrance for the park.

Ghost Lore

Sturgis is known throughout the world for the large motorcycle celebration that takes place there each year. However, located just a couple miles from Sturgis is another site visitors from all over the United States come to see. This site is called Bear Butte. The mountain is actually called a lacolith, an area that is made up of magma that never reached the surface to generate an eruption needed to form a full volcano. Although many people talk about the spirits in Sturgis, the spirits that are at Bear Butte are not of the drinking type.

- Haunted by the spirits of former inhabitants of the area.

- The mountain possesses spiritual powers that many have experienced.

- Strange unexplained noises can be heard on the mountain.

History

Geologists believe that Bear Butte was formed millions of years ago.

Artifacts that date back 10,000 years have been found in the area near Bear Butte.

1857 – Many Indian nations met at Bear Butte to discuss the encroachment of the white people.

1973 – Bear Butte was placed on the National Register of Historic Places.

2003 – The city of Sturgis was awarded a grant of $825,000 to construct a shooting range near Bear Butte.

2006 – The state of South Dakota gave back the grant money in a cloud of controversy and public outrage over the development of the site.

Investigation

This formation is not a flat–topped butte as its name would imply. The site is actually a lone mountain.

The mountain is considered to be a sacred place by many tribes. The Lakota call the site *"Mato Paha"* or Bear Mountain and the Cheyenne call it *"Noahvose."*

Numerous Native American leaders have spent time on the mountain site including Crazy Horse, Red Cloud, and Sitting Bull.

The site is believed to have gotten its name due to its unique shape. Many believe that the mountain looks like a sleeping bear that is lying on its side.

Nearly 65 different tribes regularly travel to the spiritual site to meditate, pray, and fast.

Native American lore tells of a man named Sweet Medicine traveling to the mountain to receive spiritual messages from the mountain itself. Numerous Native Americans still view the mountain as a place where the creator continues to communicate to them through visions and prayer.

Many visitors to this unique mountain report hearing strange noises while hiking through the mountain. Even after extensive searches no source of the noises can be located.

Visitors that come to experience the mountain report hearing the sounds of children playing, yet when they investigate the sounds, no children can be found.

Hikers venturing up the mountain often report hearing the mysterious sounds of dogs barking. Much to the hikers' surprise, no dogs are found.

Those who visit the sacred site report seeing the ghostly images of spirits who still inhabit the area. Often these apparitions appear to be Native Americans that disappear before the witness' eyes.

Note: *Please note that the mountain is considered to be sacred land and the park system reminds you that during your visit you will see many pieces of colored cloth and small bundles or pouches hanging from the trees. The clothes are called prayer cloths and many of the pouches contain tobacco ties that represent the prayers offered by individuals. Please respect these offerings and leave them undisturbed.*

Wounded Knee Massacre Site

Location: Wounded Knee, Shannon County, South Dakota

Directions: From Highway 18 turn north on Bigfoot Trail. Stay on the trail and the site will be on the right hand side of the road.

Ghost Lore

Perhaps no other site in America reminds us of the ugly Native American/US Government relations of the past than the Wounded Knee Memorial does. What was once an opportunity to live together in peace has become a war cry to describe pain and anger against the US Government. This small unassuming historical marker sits alone down a long dirt road forever haunting our history with the marking of the infamous massacre of 1890. For many, the marker provides a constant reminder of the hardship and struggle of the Native American, but for many others, the reminder comes directly from the victims of the massacre themselves.

- This sacred site is said to be haunted by those murdered at Wounded Knee.

- Ghostly wails continue to haunt the area.

- Overwhelming feelings of pain and sorrow radiate from the land.

History

During the 1800s, the Ghost Dance was an important part of many Native American rituals. The Ghost Dance was spread by a Paiute holy man named Wovoka. The ghost dance often consisted of a combination of meditation, chanting, dance, and prayers. However, many believed that the dance meant the earth would soon be cleansed and the "new earth" would then be given to the Indians. Others thought that by participating in the dance, they would become immune to bullets. One interesting part of this belief was that not only would the earth be given to those Native Americans who were living, but also to those who were dead.

1890 – Due to fear and misconceptions on the part of US officials the Ghost Dance was banned on the Lakota Reservations.

1890 – When Native Americans continued to perform the rites, officials panicked and called in troops to the Pine Ridge area. The troops were led by General Nelson Miles.

1890 – Soon after the panic, tribal elders moved their people to the area of the reservation known as the Stronghold. It was at the Stronghold that the elders sent word to several prominent Native American leaders including Sitting Bull to join them at the reservation.

1890 – When the white people came to disarm the group, a well respected medicine man named Yellow Bird told his people to resist them claiming the Ghost Shirts they wore would protect them from any bullets. A struggle with a Native American named Black Coyote ensued and a gun went off. This set about the tragic killing of an estimated 350 Native Americans.

1973 – Several Native American activists, upset with what they saw as racist federal policies against Native American people, seized the Wounded Knee site.

1995 – The Government looked to make Wounded Knee a National Historical Site and Park.

Investigation

The bodies of the slain Native Americans were thrown into a mass grave pit that was dug for them.

Soon after the massacre, many survivors reported hearing the wailing of the spirits of those who were killed.

Many Native Americans believe that the voices of their slain ancestors still cry out from under the soil, constantly reminding those who will listen to never forget what happened at Wounded Knee.

Those who hold beliefs in the Ghost Dance still have faith that one day their ancestors will rise from the dead and be reunited with the living.

One young man was attending a week-long gathering at Wounded Knee. During one of the warm days, the man did not feel like dancing with the group, which caused an argument with a fellow dancer. That evening the man thought a walk by himself would calm him down and give him some alone time to think over the day's events. After walking for approximately 100 yards, the man was overcome with suppressing fear, anger, despair, and pain. The sensation was so powerful, the man was nearly incapacitated. After several moments, the man was able to spin around and run towards the camp. Whatever took him over that night did not last, as the next day the young man was feeling back to normal.

Visitors to the graveyard across from the marker report seeing strange apparitions of what are believed to be the victims of the massacre.

About the Authors

Chad Lewis is a paranormal investigator for Unexplained Research LLC, with a Master's Degree in Applied Psychology from the University of Wisconsin-Stout. He has spent years traveling the globe researching ghosts, strange creatures, crop formations, werewolves, and UFOs. Chad is a former State Director for the Mutual UFO Network and has worked with BLT Crop Circle Investigations. He is the organizer of the Unexplained Conferences and the host of *The Unexplained* paranormal radio talk show.

Terry Fisk is also a paranormal investigator for Unexplained Research LLC and an authority on death and the afterlife. He is a shamanic Buddhist practitioner and member of the Foundation for Shamanic Studies who studied philosophy and religion at the University of Wisconsin. Terry is the co-host of *The Unexplained* paranormal radio talk show and director for *The Unexplained* television series.

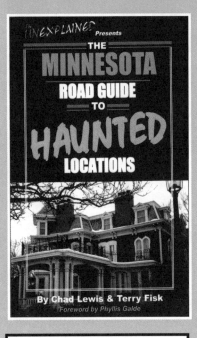